teaching reading as concept development:
emphasis on affective thinking

by
George H. Henry
University of Delaware

Bruce Tone
Editor

Ira+eic

1974
International Reading Association
800 Barksdale Road   Newark, Delaware 19711

This IRA+ERIC/CRIER publication was prepared pursuant to a contract with the U. S. Department of Health, Education, and Welfare. Contractors undertaking such projects under Government sponsorship are encouraged to express freely their judgment in professional and technical matters. Points of view or opinions do not, therefore, necessarily represent official Department of Health, Education, and Welfare position or policy.

Billie S. Strunk
Publications Editor

James L. Laffey
Director of Eric/Crier

Library of Congress Cataloging in Publication Data
Henry, George H
    Teaching reading as concept development.

    Bibliography: p.
    1. Reading   2. Concept learning.   I. Title
LB1050.H435   428'.4'07   73-85480
ISBN 0-87207-852-3

INTERNATIONAL READING ASSOCIATION

Foreword

It is a special pleasure to me as President of the International Reading Association to write the introduction to this book because it is a step forward for every language arts, reading, and literature teacher at every level of formal education.

It is relatively easy to follow established teaching practices, very hard to pioneer new ones. Once a very great scientist said to me, "I count myself lucky to have had one new idea in fifty years." We can all count ourselves lucky that George Henry had this one.

Currently, there is a great gap between Piaget's manipulative materials and the teaching of reading, a great gap between the cognitive and the affective, a great gap between the reading process and the way reading and literature are taught and tested. George Henry has provided very practical assistance at every level to put the cognitive to work for the affective, to balance comparison with contrast, to establish in the students a mind set for logical procedures in analysis and synthesis.

I am reminded of the study of achievement in literature which Alan Purves reported for the International Association for the Evaluation of Educational Achievement. He found that each country seemed to have a type of approach to literary criticism. Italy, for example, had an historical approach; the United States, a symbolic or moralistic approach. Would it be better, I wondered, to broaden the offerings so that students could develop versatility in viewing literature no matter which side of the globe they inhabit?

The author of this book has made a proposal for teaching literature which every side of the globe could use. We are indebted, of course, to him, but also to Bruce Tone, Billie Strunk, and James Laffey, who suggested that he write this book, and to IRA President Theodore Harris for authorizing it as an IRA+Eric/Crier publication.

Although I have read the book only in galley proof, I am ready to guarantee that if you make the mistake of letting it lie closed between its covers for more than a day at a time, it will sizzle. It needs constant contact with good brains. Yours.

Constance M. McCullough, *President*
International Reading Association
1974-1975

Contents

Acknowledgements

The Association gratefully acknowledges permission to use the following materials in the preparation of *Teaching Reading as Concept Development:* Excerpt from *Look Homeward, Angel* by Thomas Wolfe, copyright 1929 by Charles Scribner's Sons, reprinted by permission of Charles Scribner's Sons; "The Express" from *Selected Poems* by Stephen Spender, reprinted by permission of Random House, Inc., the publisher; "The Lake Isle of Innisfree" from *Collected Poems of William Butler Yeats,* copyright 1906 by The Macmillan Company, renewed 1934 by William Butler Yeats, reprinted by permission of The Macmillan Company; "Sea Fever" from *Poems* by John Masefield, copyright 1912 by The Macmillan Company, renewed 1940 by John Masefield, reprinted by permission of The Macmillan Company; "The Shell" from *Collected Poems of James Stephens,* copyright 1916 by The Macmillan Company, renewed 1944 by James Stephens, reprinted by permission of The Macmillan Company; "Sea Lullaby" from *Collected Poems of Elinor Wylie,* copyright 1932 by Alfred A. Knopf, Inc., reprinted by permission of Alfred A. Knopf, Inc.; "A Vagabond Song" by Bliss Carman from *Bliss Carman's Poems,* copyright by Dodd, Mead & Company, Inc., reprinted by permission of Dodd, Mead & Company, Inc.; Excerpt from *The Phenomenon of Man* by Pierre Teilhard de Chardin, copyright 1959 by Harper & Row, Publishers, Inc., reprinted by permission of Harper & Row, Publishers, Inc.; "Four Little Foxes" by Lew Sarett from *Covenant with Earth: A Selection from the Poems of Lew Sarett,* edited and copyrighted 1956 by Alma Johnson Sarett, and published 1956 by University of Florida Press, reprinted by permission of Mrs. Sarett; "The Pasture" by Robert Frost from *The Poetry of Robert Frost* edited by Edward Connery Lathem, copyright 1939, © 1967, 1969 by Holt, Rinehart and Winston, Inc., reprinted by permission of Holt, Rinehart and Winston, Inc.; "The Harbor" by Carl Sandburg from *Chicago Poems* by Carl Sandburg, copyright 1916 by Holt, Rinehart and Winston, Inc., copyright 1944 by Carl Sandburg, reprinted by permission of Harcourt Brace Jovanovich, Inc.; Excerpt from "Time and the Machine" in *The Olive Tree* by Aldous Huxley, copyright 1937 by Aldous Huxley, renewed 1965 by Laura Huxley, reprinted by permission of Harper & Row, Publishers, Inc.; Excerpt from *Critical Thinking in Reading and Writing* by Paul B. Diederich, copyright 1955 by Holt, Rinehart and Winston, Inc., reprinted by permission

□   □   □   □

I wish to thank those who aided in the making of this monograph. I
am grateful to Bruce Tone, Director of Publications for Eric/Crier,
who, after having read several articles of mine on logic in educational
method, persuaded me to turn to the study of logic in the act of
reading and offered me insightful criticism of the manuscript in
various states of its development. I appreciate, too, the help of Billie
Strunk, Publications Editor of Eric/Crier, whose advice prompted the
organization of the work. The cooperation of Faye R. Branca,
Professional Publications Editor of the International Reading Association, was helpful in both polishing the manuscript and pushing it
steadily toward publication. I also wish to thank Romayne
McElhaney, Editorial Assistant, for much kind advice in organizing
the materials. Elizabeth A. Smith, Permissions Editor, assumed responsibility for many details. I am grateful to Helen B. Ely, who, in
the midst of a busy schedule, found time to type the manuscript.

I am glad, too, that there are organizations such as the Eric
system and the International Reading Association that are willing to
sponsor pioneering and untried ideas in education.

GHH

Part one: the theory

The need for a general theory of concept development

Overemphasis on analysis of the single work

Near the end of the nineteenth century the study of the English language generally supplanted the study of Latin in our schools, or the two went side by side. The tradition of reading individual works (a poem, a story, an episode, an exposition) was carried on in imitation of the age-old practice of reading discrete classics good in themselves. That practice continues, with few exceptions, into our own time. When by the twentieth century, reading as a process became subject to research by educators and specialists, the tendency was yet to use the individual work to teach reading. Very often this was done using only a short individual passage of a work—a practice readily evident in survey anthologies and in most objective reading tests. Most basal readers are literally a collection of separate story-like episodes or individual poems taken up one by one, and teachers, by and large, teach them in this fashion.

One has only to read the literature on the teaching of reading to note a preoccupation with the skills that are entailed in reading the work singly, without relating it to other works. Of course, in teaching one work, many teachers refer pupils to something previously read and encourage them to associate it with other works with similar themes, characters, or conditions. Often such procedures are described by some reading specialists as "detecting inconsistencies between statements of different authors," "comparing the views of different authors," or "collecting data from a variety of sources."

Now there is nothing wrong about the tradition of learning to read the individual work for itself alone. To learn to cope with reading a single work in all its complexity and subtlety is fundamental eventually to reading humanistically, and from early years through high school, pupils should be slowly and steadily initiated into this kind of reading. The weakness in this method, however, is that the teaching of reading generally has stopped here.

Reading the single work has thus been identified with reading. It is generally the main goal, the end in view, from elementary school through college. Reading single works in succession is frequently a structure for particular instructional goals. Often each one is a vehicle for teaching a certain new skill; or each may advance the reader's encounter with complex organization. Successive single works may be arranged so that each is gradually more remote from the reader's literal experience. This kind of curriculum does, hopefully by the college end of it, improve the reading of the single work to the point where the instruments of literary criticism are brought into play through the interpretation and evaluation of the literary work. In such curriculi there is also the implication of shifting back and forth among the works of the growing collection read by the students to recall a work read earlier. Some teachers take satisfaction in ransacking the pupil's former reading to clarify a genre, a mode, or a literary device; but such instruction is usually "off the top of the head" and not the result of a deliberate process of reading that teaches the logical strategy of relating works.

In the middle 1930s, the pedagogical idea of correlation and integration was introduced to correct this isolation of discrete literary works from one another and from life; and the idea culminated in the unit method, wherein several works were grouped as a means of developing a certain theme close to the lives of the pupils. Many superb units were created, but in the course of time, two weaknesses emerged: 1) there was a vast overintegration to the point that pupils or teachers could cope with the complex result only superficially, and in the process, the individual work was lost sight of as a work to be carefully read; and 2) the logic of the relation of the various works to the overall theme, even when thematically focused, was generally loose and unstructured, making few demands on the pupils' reasoning powers. In other words, reading was seldom "close"—the role and use of language was skimmed over (especially when reports or panels were used) and, more particularly, any logic used went unexamined. As Blanshard (1955, p. 64) indicates, "the mere play of ideas around a topic is not reflection." The unit method did sustain interest longer and produce more discussion and more extensive reading, but the assumption within the method was that reading had already been learned, and it was now being put to work. Seemingly, by senior high school, reading did not have to be taught. So reading often became swallowed up in good talks, frequently containing little reference to the text of a work at all. Reading specialists rightly voiced their alarm.

Because of this loose emphasis on the single work within the curriculum of the language arts, pupils have not been taught to read better by relating several works into a lattice or pattern. Seldom has such a goal even been included as part of reading programs or stated as a major goal in language arts programs.

This state of affairs in reading has long continued because only during the past decade has the influence of such logicians as Russell (1913), Whitehead (1913), Carnap (1937), and Bridgman (1936) been felt in education under the names of "symbolic logic," "operationalism," and "logical behavioralism." From the base such logicians have provided, further research into how concepts are formed and attained is gradually being applied to educational methods. Particularly notable is the work of Vygotsky (1962), Bruner (1956), and Piaget (1957) and the logic of structure in Bloom (1956) and in Schwab (1961).* From all this inquiry into the nature of thought, educators may now better understand 1) how concepts are formed, 2) how concepts can be taught as an evolving set of relations eventually woven into a structure by a number of well-delineated operations, and 3) how this idea of concept development can be incorporated into the teaching of reading. As will be seen, the idea of reading as concept development now seems at last to close the gap between what has been a growing breach between those *who are reading teachers* and those *who teach literature.*

The purpose of this inquiry

These educational developments, then, underpin the twofold task of this volume: 1) to reveal how the language arts teacher at any level of instruction—from elementary school through graduate school—might go about the teaching of reading as concept development; and 2) to suggest that this method of teaching reading, if it were made part of the preparation of both the reading teacher and the English teacher, would reduce the present tension between these two areas. Concept development reveals that both areas are really one organic process—learning to read better and reading literature for appreciation.

Certain assumptions are inherent in this task. The first is that the act of reading is inextricably embedded in a thinking process, either in analysis or synthesis or in both of these processes combined. The synthesis aspect in reading has been grossly slighted, chiefly because as a process of logic it was not subject to close scrutiny until the first

---

*If the reader wishes a more detailed philosophical study of these two movements, he should read Albert Levy, *Philosophy and the Modern World.* Bloomington: Indiana University Press, 1959.

The problem of translating these fundamental sources of logic and analysis into educational theory and method is discussed in the author's study, *An Inquiry into the Nature of Concept Development Within the Ongoing Classroom Situation.* U.S. Office of Education, Project No. 1487, 1964.

decade of the century when the rise of the new logic occurred. The thinking process within synthesis can now be reduced to a set of teachable strategies or behaviors—thanks to Russell, Whitehead, Carnap, and the rise of symbolic logic. Learning these strategies through the medium of written and printed language is a way of learning to read better.

The second assumption is that the strategies inherent in either analysis or synthesis are always the same, from first grade through graduate school. It is assumed that the sole difference in reading at six or sixty is the refinement of these strategies over the years in order to assimilate more substantive matter (organized ideas). This assumption suggests and permits a spiral curriculum of logical processes. The spiral curriculum has been thought of as the yearly, sequential development of basic concepts of a discipline. We are suggesting here, instead, a year-by-year refinement and developmental mastery (control) of basic logical processes. Apparently, the behavioral goals of reading remain constant throughout the school career and life. In this sense, Göethe said that at sixty he was still learning to read.

Reading and the logic of synthesis

Reading, the new logic suggests, is the use of the modes of analysis and synthesis within the medium of written or printed language. Although analysis of the single work has been the favorite mode of reading from ancient times and is the most prevalent form of reading in our schools today, the new logic recommends the teaching of reading as synthesis. The purpose here is to show what kind of teaching of reading is entailed within the idea of reading as an act of synthesis, for understanding this relationship is necessary to the teaching of concept development. *Reading for concept development may be defined as making one's way through printed and written language in such a manner as to seek out a number of relations and to put this growing set of relations into a tentative structure.* In all synthesis, of which concept development is part, there is some interpretation, which, behaviorally stated, is the relating of two sets of relations. The pedagogical task, then, becomes this: How can we teach a pupil to relate a set of relations within the medium of printed and written language? To a large extent, this kind of relating is what reading is. The purpose here is to demonstrate what this kind of reading entails.

Establishing the theory of concept development

One part of our theory is that reading always takes place within a continuing mode of logic—not within a number of separate skills. There are two basic modes of thinking—analysis and synthesis—always present in reading. Both are intertwined whether a work is read singly or in relation to another work.

Two modes of thought: synthesis and analysis

Let us briefly review the act of analysis as it pertains to reading—just to delineate sharply what kind of reading this study is not dealing with primarily. Whenever we break up a work or passage into parts, we are analyzing. In analysis we always aim to separate for some definite reason, for some goal. We may separate form from content; and in turn form may be further subdivided—the story form, for instance, into setting, plot, characters, theme, style; or plot may be cut into interrelated episodes, such as introduction, rising action, climax, conclusion; or rhetoric may be broken into image, figure, symbol; or we may teach the pupil to look at the work from separate levels: the psychological, the sociological, or the structural. In exposition, too, the pupil is often asked to find the main points and to separate from them their method of development. We all like to have pupils do this sort of analytical thinking when they read. This analytical process has become our main way of teaching reading for appreciation and for comprehension. Our justification is that in time the pupil may do this kind of dissection on his own, and above all, analysis may reveal to him how the work as an entity was put together by the author or, rather, what holds the work together. All this is assumed in the faith that awareness of a work's "art" will lead pupils to more enjoyment and understanding. Also, such study may open the possibility for more perceptual engagement in the work. In the hands of special reading teachers, reading of this kind has become almost equivalent to reading itself.

Some teacher might protest that in his classes the foregoing elements of a work emerge by means of induction and that induction is surely a mode of synthesis. This is true: the parts or separated elements of a literary work may be arrived at by having the pupils strive for a definition of the part (say, the climax) from several examples. The main purpose or ultimate end of this use of the process of induction is to achieve an empirical concreteness, to understand (set limits to) a part—the part of a story called setting—after looking at a number of settings in various stories. This process is better than furnishing the pupils with an experientially empty definition of setting prepared beforehand by the teacher.

In short, analysis is mostly deductive, in that one cannot separate what is not already given or believed to be already inherent. Separation can be a highly creative process; for instance, the first time Vitamin C was separated out, the process entailed more than deduction because it hypothesized a part of a whole and then a testing to see whether it was there. We often call this kind of separation a "discovery."

It is to be recognized then that a certain amount of synthesis goes on within the analysis of parts—whether it is of a story, a novel, or a poem. For example, two characters may be compared, the plot may be related to the theme, or a setting may be related to a motivation. But the overall function of this kind of teaching—whether by induction or deduction—is the *analysis* of a single work: what it is, what it is like, what its parts are. Analysis is the controlling operation. The pupils are brought to analyze the work to understand how the author synthesized it. Two diagrams may clarify the point.

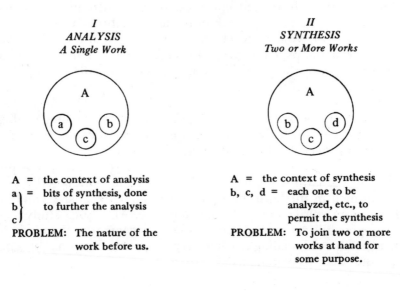

I
ANALYSIS
A Single Work

A = the context of analysis
a ⎫
b ⎬ = bits of synthesis, done to further the analysis
c ⎭

PROBLEM: The nature of the work before us.

II
SYNTHESIS
Two or More Works

A = the context of synthesis
b, c, d = each one to be analyzed, etc., to permit the synthesis

PROBLEM: To join two or more works at hand for some purpose.

Teaching reading as concept development

It is the reading growing out of model II that will be demonstrated here. Reading as in model I has overwhelmed the instructional act to the extent that there has been little exploration into the kind of reading instruction needed for doing the work of model II. One reason for this condition is that our academic ideal of extreme specialization has almost solely encouraged analysis for well over a hundred years, until knowledge has become fragmentized and chaotically pluralistic with its many disciplines left dangling. Few scholars build comprehensive views even of their own discipline. And our academic culture does not expect us to do so in the classroom. For this reason White (1955) has called our culture *The Age of Analysis.*

Analysis and *synthesis* are Greek terms still reserved for the two large modes of logic. Our commonplace words for these are *separating* and *joining* (Anglo-Saxon, *yoking*). One of these operations can never go on without the other, but one of them is always in the ascendency only because of our purpose. Logical purpose is an organizing drive. Analysis (separating) encases synthesis (joining) when we want (purpose) to get at the nature of something, a poem or a story. We may analyze a sample of water for typhoid germs or for mercury; we may analyze a sentence to see whether there is a direct object or an adverb clause. On the other hand, synthesis supersedes and embodies analysis when we want to put together into a whole several separate parts or separate relations of a work (poems or stories). To do so, we must construct or invent or design. Writing a sentence of one's own is an act of synthesis; so is writing a paragraph and so is a certain kind of reading. Suppose the class has read four stories in succession, each making a certain impact. This question should arise (but seldom does): What do they all mean as a total experience? The task as logic is: How could we put them all together? Synthesis is demanded by such a question. In life we continually have experiences, one after the other, sometimes several simultaneously; and we have not only to meet them as separate encounters but also eventually to put them somewhere inside one or alongside other experiences—to associate them, relate them, or incorporate them. Merely to pile them up—to store them heterogeneously—is to live a life of unthinking busyness, which means eventually to lose stability. Thus, for a pupil to read in class each day for months a collection of discrete works is, ironically, to court meaninglessness, even while gaining numerous separate meanings by an analysis of a host of books read singly in daily succession. In life we either intuitively or consciously ask ourselves, "Is a pattern developing, or a trend—for instance, a decline of the war, an increase in the cost of living, a recession?" Psychologically, we may ask, "Is this event another instance of *my* failure or an exception?" Growth is synthesis. Much pre-analysis is necessary before synthesis can take place, but the outcome, the product, the decision, the plan, the attitude, the meaning that the pupil invents—each of these is a set of relations, a structure that the pupil puts together. All are modes of synthesis.

Probably the best distinction between the two large modes of logic is that although one must include the other, within the context of analysis, the synthesis or joining done is small-scale and is performed for the sake of separation, which is to say the understanding of parts—how they fit together. We can try to separate two leaves in respect to species, or separate two vast concepts like God and nature in respect to man. Even when the parts are put together again—for instance, having the pupils read the whole poem once more after it has been dissected—we have only a restoration, a fitting back together of parts, not a synthesis. Putting parts together, therefore, may not be a synthesis; it may lead only to a collection or a summary.

In contrast, in the mode of synthesis we must rely on many separate small-scale analyses, not only to get more out of the individual work but also to perform a joining with another work external to it—external by reason of its seemingly different form or separate existence. In synthesis the pupil is not restoring what he took apart; he is making something not there until he synthesized it. Of course, in order to teach him the nature of synthesis, we can show him some syntheses others have done; but caution must be exercised in that the pupil is then not synthesizing at all, only analyzing another's synthesis.

Throughout the academic world there is an assumption that by constant, continual analysis, the student will learn somehow to read for synthesis. The reason for this is that nearly all language arts teachers and nearly all reading teachers have sat in classes either watching and hearing professors primarily analyze works or, under the professor's sway, performing analysis on their own. Seldom is synthesis broached, even when several literary theories lie side by side unassimilated. And, if synthesis is tried at all, the professor nearly always does it himself or refers the students to a source (a critic or a scholar) where it has been done. No wonder so little comprehensive synthesis is taught to our young, for neither language arts teachers nor reading teachers have had much experience with it in their own reading. Practice is gained through writing a term paper for which one has to read several works. Too many term papers, however, merely bring together or assemble the syntheses of their sources without interpretating them.

Concept development as a form of synthesis

Concept development, then, as the new logic uses it, is an act of synthesis. Behaviorally, synthesis is a joining or a relating of things seemingly existing separately; or if they do exist apart, their separate existence depends on a relation. Synthesis is a discovery of the nature of that relation. There are all kinds of joining, from the fitting of two pipes by a plumber to the ceremony of marriage in which two people become "one flesh." Grouping, comparing, and generalizing are other forms of joining. We may join the moon and the earth, both of which, however distant and distinct, may from a certain point of view be said to be one system. The conditions of this oneness would have to be explained and demonstrated; that is, relations would have to be discovered and a structure of these relations invented. These two would *be* the system. The system *is* the synthesis.

The intuitive element in synthesis. Each discovery of relation and each creation of structure has something of the investigator (the pupil) in its being: the person's originality, his flash of insight. In synthesis, man makes what is not there until synthesized. Of two books, the comparison is not *in* either of the books; it is invented. A teacher can point out for the pupil the elements in each book to be related, or he may put before the student the discoveries of other readers and how each made his way to the discovery. In time, and with practice, the pupil may come to deal skillfully with relating; but he must do it steadily for himself or he cannot become good at it.

Because scholars are often quite creative and original, their synthesis leads again and again to failure; but failure leads to fresh perceptions, other strategies. It is the creativity that may result from failure that we do not teach our pupils when they read badly. Richards (1938) also brings this out: "Misunderstanding, then . . . is no crime. If it is not actually to be welcomed, it is at least an opportunity for teaching . . . . " If the teacher constantly deals with ready-made synthesis in the teaching of reading and if he synthesizes *for* the student, he denies the pupil the opportunity to gain the temerity and the adventure of running ahead of analysis, which he must do to read creatively.

Only after he has broken up (separated out, analyzed) each of two or more works is a reader able to bring the two together with meaning. But the purpose in bringing any two literary works together is outside either of the literary works, and the quality of fulfilling that purpose does not exist solely in the works but partly in the person who is to do the synthesis.

Concept development as a form of synthesis comprises two acts: 1) the discovery of relation and 2) the invention of structure. Each of these acts can be further divided into a set of strategies that can be taught to a pupil in such a way that the pupil combines and joins ideas while reading. (How this is done in the teaching of reading we will describe later, for we wish here to establish the theory.) In contrast, there is a discovery of relation in analysis that already exists but that does not move toward the invention of structure. Having pupils trace the internal structural relations of a work in the manner of the new criticism, which until recently has been a favorite device of English teachers, is very much within the realm of analysis. In this kind of reading, the pupil does not need to build a relation or create a structure; he ever seeks parts. The new criticism does insist, however, that no amount of analysis *is* the poem. Analysis, however, may aid and instigate either one of the two acts. For instance, when a pupil reexamines or rereads the text in order to make sure he is picking out and writing down the main points, he is analyzing. But when this same act is done to relate these main points to other main points in another book in order to find a place for them in a growing structure, it becomes a strategy in synthesis.

The discovery of relation. The phrase *discovery of relation* identifies a type of logical discovery. The term *discovery,* like so many terms borrowed from other disciplines, has become ambiguous in pedagogy and, of course, in reading. Discovery has been used to justify the stuffiest kind of activity, such as looking things up in the library to find a specific fact. Discovery, as used in concept development, is part of a logical process. In analysis, discovery is the act of isolating, of picking out, of selecting; the isolation *is* the discovery—for example, identifying radium or penicillin. But in synthesis we ask: Where does radium go among the other elements? How does it relate within the interplay of these elements? How, now that it is found, does it modify the structure of relations of the elements? How does it alter the meaning of *element* itself?

The answers to such questions involve structures of relations. By relating relations, one evolves to a concept. Thus, if one wishes to create a concept, one must discover relations and how they are themselves related. And development of a concept is an organizing activity which entails strategies of thinking, as we shall see.

Even a very small-scale relation may be a discovery. Suppose the pupil has read two works and has analyzed each of them in the customary literary way. Suppose he is now asked to relate the two works in light of some purpose. This new logical demand will require him to run over or reanalyze each once more. This time, however, he

Teaching reading as concept development

will analyze each for a different purpose—to discover how to put them together. What kind of relation will it be? He does not look up the answer somewhere. He must relate and know the nature of the relationship. In an act of logical discovery, the pupil himself must create something not *in* both, yet *of* both. The quality of the synthesis will depend more on the skill of his reanalysis than on that of his initial analysis of each work. At the same time, it will depend on the kind of strategies he employs in the act of relating the two reanalyses. In other words, analysis for the sake of separating is not the same as analysis for the sake of combining. We find something else—something more—in the second kind of analysis because we read the selection with a specific aim—to combine it with some other analyzed selection in the light of our purpose. This defines operationally what we may call the logic of purpose.

Affective influences. It is important to note that one need not teach reading with thinking as its only end. Reading for synthesis is always a creative act, in that what comes out of the joining goes beyond what is in any of the elements of the material read. The result resides in the assimilated skill of the person performing the strategies of synthesis and also in the play of his imagination and his intuition. Bruner (1960) believes that intuition and imagination, since they are qualities of mind within cognition, should be stimulated, even to encouraging the pupil to make intelligent guesses. It is possible to train for intuition by allowing it to be exercised, but many teachers dislike it because initially it necessarily leads to clumsy, dismaying results—to something labeled failure. They fail to understand how this bungling can be made part of creativity in reading. Synthesis in reading implies a search for connectedness—a seeking to reconcile, to unify, to organize, to establish significance—or as Whitehead (1929) puts it, "to move toward concretion." He writes, "Creativity is the principle of novelty . . . . The ultimate metaphysical principle is the advance from disjunction to conjunction, creating a novel entity other than the entities given in disjunction." Reading as concept development should be taught in a manner that fosters the intuition and imagination necessary for discovery, which, to Whitehead, is the effort through cognition to combine disjunctions.

This process of concretion should not be pure thought devoid of feeling. Both analysis and synthesis in the English classroom and in the reading clinic too often lapse into sheer dry-bone cognition. The work of art is organic—an affective experience put in such a form by its creator that it is potentially fused to explode by a spark from the reader. In art, readiness is all; the engagement is everything. But even analysis of reaction or response, although good for the pupil, steadily presses the juices of feeling out of the response. An epiphany, an encounter, as a form of response is in itself an inchoate organic synthesis. Only when we ask what the shaft of light that struck us is and how it struck us are we analyzing. On the other hand, when we probe our several successive encounters with literary works to seek out what is happening to us as we accrue their experience or what they mean in total, we are synthesizing. Both modes of thought reduce the tension of response. The pedagogical problem is not so much how to sustain the tension while the synthesis is going on, as how to keep the pupil at the inquiry when the tension has subsided. This interplay of the affective and the cognitive in reading as concept development will be gone into later on. Concept development should always be done within experience, not for itself. This means that a teacher should never teach thinking solely by making pupils think. Yet there are straight reading classes and reading clinics that have such a rigid and narrow conception of reading for comprehension (seeking main points and subpoints) that they rule out the reading of stories, poems, and plays. Thus they ignore most of the pupil's experiences that may be a resource for reading comprehension. Unfortunately, many clinics teach reading with no play on the affective appeal of their materials even when they do use plays, stories, and poems.

The writer has forty-five videotapes of English teaching wherein the affective domain is well-nigh negligible in the treatment of literature, and wherein synthesis is not used at all to relate the various feelings of students.

The experential, affective mode can be carried on without any conceptual processes, it must be noted. One exciting fifth grade experience unit was structured around the topic, "The Mouse." Consciously built into it was every conceivable language activity—writing scenes to be acted, manipulating mouse puppets, listening to recordings of stories created by pupils, reading books from a list of 20, watching movie cartoons, writing compositions, displaying drawings and creative objects, taking notes on actual mice, reciting poems, and looking up unknown facts about real mice—all that the progressives of the 1920s called the lush environment and that the neo-progressives of the 1960s called the free, open-ended classroom. But something was lacking. There was little conscious conceptualization—no discovered relations, no invention of structure, no sustained comparisons, no conflicting ideas to be resolved, no evaluation of the behavior of mice, no categories to be created. Experience was all. Of course, such mental activities did occur naturally, but only incidentally and unconsciously. The teacher, if made aware of the pedagogical situation, could have changed the organization of the unit from a topic around which language experiences rotated to a concept to be developed in several dimensions—all without any loss of interest, any inhibition of activity, or any impairment of spontaneity. The pupils would have had still another display: an achieved structure of thought, ironically growing out of many wide ranging experiences.

What concept development entails at its best is something such as this from T. S. Eliot's *Dry Savages*:

> We had the experience but missed the meaning, and approach to the meaning restores the experience in a different form . . . .

The role of relation and structure. So far, we have been explaining the nature of synthesis in concept development and how synthesis has a creative or novel element in it. Let us now return in more detail to the two basic elements in concept development.

1] *The discovery of relation.* Relation entails the many acts of joining. It is always a discovery in seeing something that was not at first seen—a combining that was not thought possible or a pursuit of an anticipated union in spite of differences. This discovery is never contained in just one of the several works that are joined. A number of strategies can be identified that are necessary to this act of relating. To teach these strategies through language is to teach reading as relation; these strategies may guide synthesis but may not, as was pointed out above, insure its quality. Relating is the first step in concept development, and comparing is one process of relating. Comparison as relating, for example, may look like this:

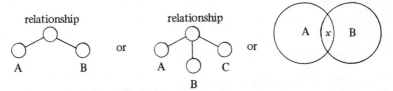

These will be explained and developed later within the context of teaching reading.

2] *The invention of structure.* A structure is a set of discovered relations—a joining of combinations. Piaget (1957) pictures this logical process as a lattice. We *invent* a lattice because what is erected is not in the several relations being joined, each relation being held together by a level of abstraction that we ourselves must invent. Here are inventions at differing levels of abstraction:

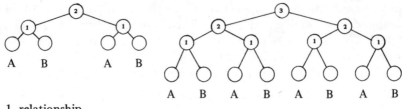

1. relationship
2. relationship of relationships
3. more general relationship

Some reading texts prefabricate the structure (lattice in figure) and lead the pupil through it by the hand, so to speak, still calling it *discovery* and *invention*. But the teacher using such texts has taken the relations and the structure from the text or its workbook. There is little discovery or invention for the pupil in such a case or when the relations and structures are relayed from a borrowed unit or perhaps a set of questions from an anthology. This process is not concept development because the pupil does not himself seek a relation or himself build a structure of relations. Traditionally, the prepared lesson structured by the teacher is the method of rationalism, a pedagogy well practiced in Greek days and holding sway down through the *Age of Reason* even to our own time in texts on reading and in college syllabi. But this is not creative discovery or invented structure within the pupil's act of reading.

This overteaching of ready-made structures throughout the elementary and secondary schools has been drying up the pupil's imagination, his inclination for intuition, his cultivation of feeling, his existential force to create by means of reading. Concept development, in contrast, is a way to familiarize the pupil with the strategies of synthesis; inherent in it are imagination, interpretation, meaning.

The logical process of conceptualization

To conceptualize means to discover relations and to invent a structure of these relations. The act of discovery comes before the act of structuring, else there would be nothing to structure. Both the process of relating and the process of structuring consist of a number of operations, but structure is different from relation in that it relates *relations* by the use of levels of abstraction (see figure). In the logic of Russell and Whitehead (1910-1913), developing a relation implies four fundamental operations that are constantly being intertwined. Actually, one cannot be used without the others. Here is my condensation of these operations:

1] *The act of joining* (bringing together, comparing, generalizing, classifying). Its logical operator is *and* (*moreover, fur-*

Teaching reading as concept development

thermore). Its grammatical form is the coordinating conjunction and the connective abverb.

2] *The act of excluding* (discriminating, negating, rejecting). Its logical operator is *not* (*this . . . not that*). Its grammatical form *neither . . . nor* (exclusive, dichotomous).

3] *The act of selecting* (one or the other or both). Its logical operator is *some* (*part, few*). Its grammatical form is *either . . . or*; quantitative pronouns.

4] *The act of implying* (*if* not *this . . . then that*; cause-effect, result, necessity, proof, condition). Its logical operator is *if . . . then*. Its grammatical form is the subordinating connective abverb and the subordinating conjunction.

These operations* are necessary in order to seek a relation or to structure a number of relations. Their instantaneous intertwining, even among slow pupils, goes on continuously when reading takes place. Without such activity, in fact, there can be no reading. In the teaching of literature and of grammar, these operators (*if, and, or, not*) are nearly always restricted to their grammatical function in syntax rather than treated as logical strategies. Bridgman writes of them in this way: "The meaning of such words is usually taken as intuitively known and they are therefore treated as unanalyzed in any logical enterprise. This does not mean, however, that they are incapable of analysis or that we should not try to analyze them." (p.95) The pedagogical problem is to make youth feel at home with these operations within the medium of language. Language as a medium for these four operations often gives youth trouble because all youth (even the bright) have a limited control of language.

All of us use the operations for relating whenever we think. Yet to Whitehead and Russell, these four operations do not describe thinking: they are mind, and their interplay is thinking. Recent studies show that a baby begins them almost immediately. They do not need to be taught; rather, they need to be exercised in all sorts of ways and situations with verbal symbols and language forms. Put in another way, exercising them is learning, and school is a place to provide experiences which exercise them, requiring the kind of verbal combinations that would generally not be picked up by the pupil elsewhere. They supply us with a more explicit definition of reading for concept development: *Reading for concept development is the*

---

*Piaget (1957, p. *X*) puts them this way:
  1. not (negation)
  2. and (conjunction)
  3. or (disjunction—either or both)
  4. if . . . then (implication)

exercise of joining, excluding, selecting, and implying within written symbols—that is, within syntax, rhetoric, and literary form.

In time, reading becomes second nature in that the medium of language seems transparent; and the four operations go on much like breathing. The more the arbitrary symbolism of language is understood and used and the more the above four operations are consciously exercised, the better the pupil learns to read intuitively. The excellent reader is one who senses how the language as medium works upon the thought and how the logical operators in turn make use of the language to attain one's purpose. This interplay constitutes the art of reading—handling the symbols (language) as one would handle a piano or a guitar, developing concepts through the operators as one would play the notes. But the analogy is not quite good enough; good reading is more like continually tuning or stringing the guitar while playing it: we test the ideas as they develop. That is why critical reading is very difficult.

These four operations always take place in any logical process, whether it be comparison, induction, evaluation, deduction, analysis, or validation. The purpose of a logical process is to organize these operations in such a way as to lead to a structure of relations. This emergence of a structure *is* the concept. Reading as concept development has for its aim the invention of a set of relations.

These four logical operations assume such common sense names as uniting (coordinating), separating (contrasting), selecting (omitting), and involving (predicting, causing). Each weaves into all the others. For example: in the simple act of uniting, one must also discard (separate) some items after an evaluation of the item to be united (involving); for to discard is to isolate (negate) by an evaluative selection. Next, one examines the element selected for union in order to find a place for it in the combination (classification); thus, this positive act of selecting an item for union with another item also embodies an implication (if not this to be combined, then that). Now enters probability: how certain is the choice of the two items to be joined, how strong is the sequence or relation between them (cause and effect)? The total movement of these operations is the logical process in the discovery of relation and the invention of structure called classifying. Blanshard (1955) phrases this intertwining in this way: "Distinction, identification, and classification all occur together." (p. 542) The pupil's manipulation in this way of some concept (to him inchoate) changes his original meaning of the concept: a change of meaning or extending a meaning is the definition of development. A concept is a structure of relations continually growing.

Let us illustrate the operations of relating in the act of reading by first considering the relations in two relatively demanding prose passages. The first must be analyzed alone, of course.

The Roar Of A Great City

The electric light, the telephone and telegraph wires have added new music to our city. When the winds blow at night one can hear a somber, melancholy music high up in the air—as mysterious as that of Ariel himself or the undiscovered music of the Pascagoula. If you want to hear it in perfection go some of these windy nights we have lately enjoyed to Delord or Dryades, or some of the streets in the neighborhood of the electric-light works, where the wires are numerous and the houses low, and where there is a clean sweep for the wind from the New Basin to the river. There the music becomes wild and grand indeed. The storm whistling and shrieking around some sharp corner never equaled it. Above, around, in every direction can be heard this music, sighing, mourning like the treetops, with a buzzing metallic sound that almost drowns your conversation. There is something in it weird and melancholy—it is like the last wail of a dying man, or the shriek of the angel of death as he clasps his victim to him.

If such it is today, what have we to hope for in the future? If the city is already a monstrous spiderweb, a great Aeolian harp, what is its destiny with several new telephone and telegraph companies, and thousands of new poles, and millions of new wires promised us. If this aerial music increases, this shrieking and moaning and wailing will reach such a pitch that we will greet the rattle of the floats and tinkle of the streetcars as tending to drown the new noise, and welcome the roar of the city as likely to muffle its meaning.

— Lafacadio Hearn

Before we take up this prose passage, the reader ought first to read it his way. One suspects that the reader will do what nearly all of us do—young and old, with varying degrees of education. We read at our own pace, finish with an inchoate lump of meaning unformed by language, and then go on to other reading or nonreading activity. Only when we try to communicate the ideas of the passage to ourselves or to others or to relate it to another work or passage do we determine what meaning is really ours. We may find that what we thought we read is not there; or, most likely, in the very telling, we may revise our idea of the passage. This is especially probable if we check our thought by rereading parts of the passage. Generally, what we possess of it lies inert, subject to attrition, unless we try to explain to others what we hold and/or to relate it to some other passage we have read or to some other experience we have had. In short, we must conceptualize it—join it to something. That is, we must synthesize it, which always entails bringing something of ourselves to it. The conclusion for teaching, it would seem, is that reading is inextricably tied up with both oral and written composition, with experience, with other concepts inside us, and with other reading.

In light of an ultimate reading for synthesis, then, how would we have the pupil read this prose passage? First, there must be an initial analysis which should encourage the pupil to trace the kind of logic that holds the thought together. The reading is not to be only a matter of proceeding solely with so-called reading skills like "finding the main idea," "picking out supporting details," "seeking relations" (when the search is vague and not logical), "bringing one's experience to the reading," or "hunting for the topic sentence." None of these—either in itself or with the others—really constitutes a logical process. Nor should the reading proceed through the kind of broad questions that English teachers are fond of—questions that often do not invite much cognitive challenge or a close rereading: "What is the author trying to tell us? What does this passage mean? What is your reaction? Discuss the passage." Such questions often evoke the kind of spontaneous discussion of the reading that we all hope for, but the discussion is often without the logic or process necessary to hold the pupil's thoughts together. As a result, the thoughts of the classroom are hardly distinguishable from those produced in a casual dormitory bull session. Such free discussions may later be a means of embarking on the conceptualization of the passage. But to read for concept development, we must go beyond exercising these "skills" and answering such broad questions, to a focused, logical quest.

Actually, the conventional reading skills that have dominated the teaching of reading for decades do not get at the basic logical processes operating in a passage or work such as that by Hearn. In analyzing that passage, a very strong reader would hardly ask himself, "What is the main idea and what are the subordinating ideas or supporting points?" He would trace the sequences of thoughts—what the author is doing logically—and from this he would sense the totality of aim. Intuitively, he would trace how the author joins, selects, discards, and implies and entails ideas. Surely, the young sophomore in high school, even if a fairly good reader, would have trouble and would really be bewildered by so general a directive as "Find the main point." Nor does the familiar exercise of outlining a passage or story or novel penetrate the progression of ideas and their interlacing. Such a task becomes so broad that it suggests no "thought" behavior—neither an operation nor a process—to help the pupil discern what logically is going on in the passage. The logical skeleton of the quoted passage may be analyzed in this way:

1] There is a continuous joining of various specific sounds of a city (other sounds had to be deliberately discarded). The sounds were so selected and joined as to form a class of sounds that together may be called eerie and unnatural. This invented class of sounds is what in common sense terms we call a general impression. In logic, the impression is a generalization.

2] There is an implication (if this . . . then that) drawn from the impression or generalization, from this new set of sounds for the future city. Given these peculiar kinds of sounds held together by the more general idea of a roaring city, then something can be predicted for the future city. This is a deduction.

3] This prediction (an implication) takes the form of a prophecy. The prophecy is intuitively implied from the general condition or impression created in paragraph one. The implication is not here subject to proof. It comes as a warning of what might happen.

The young reader should come to see that two main operations are in progress here: the creation of a condition concerning the city by the act of selection (a judicious joining and an inductive discarding to form a generalization) and the drawing of an implication from the created condition. The two logical processes are means of establishing the concept: the roar may eventually blot out its own meaning. But how can we get the pupils to feel the brilliance of this paradox?

The reading is not really finished. A critical reading relooks at the act of joining and the act of implication. For the pupil to state only the conceptual relation between roar and city—to pick it out—is not fully to conceptualize the passage.

4] The pupils ought first to attempt to interpret the logical skeleton: Is it true? How well is the implication grounded in the generalization? Is the generalization adequate in light of the selected details? Is the selection of the details accurate; that is, were too many other details discarded or overlooked in order to gain the generalization?

5] Next there ought to be an interpretation (a move to a higher abstraction) of its substance: Is technology an unmixed blessing? Is technology making city life more and more meaningless?

The above cognitive appraisal is only one level of reading. The literary or aesthetic dimension needs to be explored: choice of adjectives, freshness of metaphor, the subtle use of classic myth, the cumulative thrust of the paradox. Besides, the feeling or tone of the passage is perhaps central to the reading. The logic and the literary organization of the passage together create our conceptualization of it.

The process of reading that we have been describing here is, of course, analysis. Only number five moves toward synthesis, after the analysis. Our purpose is to show that reading by analysis can also be improved if the vaguely phrased reading skills are replaced by attention to specific reading behavior (the four operators). Since ours is an investigation into reading as an act of synthesis, however, it would be a digression to expand and deepen the idea of analysis at this point. The pupils, let us assume, now have some idea of the logic and the idea of this passage. What should the teacher do with what they have learned? Should he just stop and go on to another discreet work, doing much the same thing? This is the usual method.

Of course, we do not propose putting youth inflexibly through these five algorithmic steps of analysis. The logic of the passage has been depicted here for the teacher. But, by an awareness of the process of conceptualization in teaching, the teacher should be able to teach reading better than by the conventional reading skills approach or by merely provoking the "lively and good discussion" of the all-out experience approach so common now to English teachers influenced by the free classroom.

Suppose, instead of dropping the passage to make way for another work on another theme, which is the usual method, the teacher would next pursue with the pupils the idea of evaluating technology. To do this, the teacher may now put another passage about technology before the pupils, asking them first to sift it and analyze it in much the same way they treated the first passage, and then determine how it may shed light on the reading of the previous passage. Actually, the analysis of passage two, by its sheer proximity to passage one, will intuitively be affected by what trace or residue the pupil brings from passage one and then joins, perhaps unconsciously, to the analysis of passage two. In addition, there will be a closer and different reading of passage one on the return to it because the goal of the task of reading now becomes one of the synthesis of the two passages.

The Man With A Tractor

Usually Sank was just an ordinary-looking man, just an average-looking farmer, with arms and legs, a mouth and eyes, a wife and two children. Working there in that barn, the wind howling outside, in the dim half-light, with that gas mask on, and the rats scurring around, he didn't look like a farmer. He looked like a product of a more advanced civilization. He didn't even look like a man. He looked like some horrible, sightless, anthropoidal thing with a snout.

He scooped the golden grain and it was hard work. He didn't quit until he had put it all through the machine. Then he threw down the scoop, cut off the motor, took off his gas mask, and went to the house. He

Teaching reading as concept development

noticed the thin row of young Chinese elms again. Last year the sap-
lings had bent flat to the ground before the force of the onslaught. This
year the Chinese elms were not bowing their heads quite so low. Next
year . . . .

The wind had subsided as suddenly as it had struck. Sank went out and
unhitched his plow, hitched the tractor to the drill, set the sprockets of
the drill so that it would sow twenty pounds to the acre, and scooped
the seed wheat into the drill bins until they were level full. He oiled and
watered and fueled the tractor and lubricated both tractor and drill.
Then he lowered the disks, cranked the tractor, threw it into fourth
speed, and took off up the edge of the plowed field, making four miles
an hour, sowing wheat.

Wheat is undoubtedly the finest, most courageous thing that grows on
the face of the earth. The implement drilled the seed wheat into the
earth. If I were called upon to award the first prize to the best thing
that grows, I should walk up and hand the gold medal over the head of
a stalk of hard winter wheat. The disks made little planting furrows; the
drill set down the single grains of wheat in the furrows; the drag-chains
covered them over with soil. It was all mechanical. It was different from
the days, from Joseph down to not so long ago, when a man dipped
into a sack of seed wheat and sowed it by hand, three scattering throws
to the handful.

— Morrow Mayo

Again, first by analysis, let us look at what is going on here in
logical terms. As we noted before, the skills approach of the conventional workbook exercises does not get the reader into the logic of
the passage. Going over the four paragraphs, a pupil would hardly
know how to look for what is main and what is subordinate, where
the inferences are, and what the sequences are. In most workbooks,
the terms *inference* and *sequence,* as molar skills, carry little behavioral denotation.

With questioning directed toward the logic of the passage, the
teacher can guide the pupils toward the use of the four operators.
For example, "How did the author describe Sank?" The answer to
this question would not be the actual descriptive phrases as such, but
would come through the process of logic—two exclusions and a
union by means of a figure of speech: not a farmer, not a man, but
like a thing with a snout. "Notice the contrast (an *or* suggestion) in
paragraph two," the teacher might say. "What is its purpose? This is
the first time that nature is brought in as being different from technology. Are they opposites? Why did Sank go in? There is considerable joining in paragraph three—to what end? Why does he bring
together wheat and wind? Do both belong to nature? Yet how do
they differ? How is the wheat related to the steps in mechanical
planting? All the thought in paragraph four moves to a generalization. What is it? In what logical form? Is the mechanization on man's

side or on nature's side?" All the preceding questions are in the mode of analysis.

What is the logical skeleton of the passage?

1] Mechanization has reached the barn of the farm.

2] The combinations of detail form a contrast (a separation), mechanization and the threat of nature—the wind and the elms. This is subtly handled: the wind could halt the mechanical devices.

3] The mechanization of sowing in the field (its details combined in a functional order) aids the eternal wheat.

4] "It was all mechanical": this generalization establishes a contrast with hand sowing—a separation which here points up evolutionary progress.

As in the previous passage, the literary qualities like imagery, the figures of speech, the poetic praise of wheat, the concrete detail culminating in the phrase, "It is all mechanical" are rhetorical aspects of the passage, not necessary to its logic, but contributing to the emotional effect.

Interpretation: synthesis as the relating of generalizations

When we begin a synthesis of the two works, the determining influence of a context must be kept in mind. Suppose, with the help of the pupils, we adopt as a directive context the evaluation of technology. This means behavioristically that certain aspects of passage one may guide the rereading of passage two. We now ask, "What kind of synthesis can be projected?" As we read, the feeling in the tone of the first passage toward technology is clearly one of doubt; the second passage, not obviously devoid of apprehension, suggests the optimism of progress.

1] The tractor and the drill are welcomed as progress without apprehension.

2] The "next year . . . " suggests uncertainty created more by arbitrary nature than by a mechanical backlash.

3] Mechanization has come to the farm, but the idea of farming as an industry is not developed here.

4] There is no larger context: the passage does not deal with where the oil comes from and how it gets to the farm, the urban manufacture of iron and steel, the assembly line that produces the tractor and drill, and the farm's dependence on technology from the industrial city.

Teaching reading as concept development

The prophecy (the implication of the first passage) and the generalization of the second passage are seemingly disjunctive. Are they mutually exclusive? The pupils should be made aware that separating—as can be done here—is a relation. Is there no way of combining them? Some pupil may try to reconcile the two by reducing them to two aspects of one problem—technology in the city and technology on the farm. The farm is now dependent on the city for electricity, oil refining, and steel and iron; but this idea is in neither passage.

The passages together, but not singly, point to the pervasive influence of technology in our culture. In each passage, nature is thought of differently. In the first, technology seems to be outrivaling the foreboding darkness of night and the whining wind, even transcending the imagination inherent in ancient myths. In the second, nature, poetically conceived, is feared for its power (the destructive Dust Bowl wind) but is also praised (the eternal germination of wheat). Thus technology seems a benign extension of man's hand and a way of overcoming or working with nature.

In trying to join the two passages (*and*), one must first separate them (*or*) in various ways of differentiation: *A* (in the city), *B* (in the country). *A* includes the increasing development of electricity and *B*, the mechanization of the farm. Held up separately in this way, the two passages seem so far apart that no commonality of importance can be detected. How could a joining be effected? Both deal with advancing technology but each quite differently (a negation?). Could it be that technology is melting down the concepts rural and urban? *A* looks upon technology in light of future consequences, with some awesome doubt; *B* looks at technology from a backward stance, ancient hand sowing, thus with a sense of progress. In *A*, the practicality of electricity is lost sight of; in *B*, the practicality of the tractor is gently accepted. In *A*, nature (night) is not thought of as an opponent; in *B*, the lurking demon Nature (windstorms) seems ever there.

The young reader must come to see that the idea of technology in itself is an inadequate joiner or synthesis of the two because it is so concrete as to contribute little to our understanding unless some more abstract idea like "the pervasive march of technology" be the joiner, through which our purpose may be to reveal the simultaneous nature of the march—in both city and country, and thus its interlocking relation.

The pupils must be aware that in this kind of synthesis they are going beyond what is actually and literally before them in the two passages. What is the justification for going beyond? It can be found only in the two together by means of the directing purpose created and established for their union. The teacher must keep in mind that a synthesis is not an assemblage of particulars, not a synopsis.

Among all pupils, even among the good readers, the main weakness in all attempts at synthesis is the tendency to settle for concrete and superficial elements or ideas. It is no synthesis to say that two novels have murder in common, or two poems have the sea in common, or two stories have love in common. Pupils, therefore, need training in joining elements or works with abstract relations pertinent to the purpose for which they are being joined.

Of course, these two passages were written independently, and not meant to be reconciled. But they do exist, quite separately as entities, and in reading both together we are probing for a common intrinsic attitude or idea, if it can be found; in this case, an evaluation of technology. The pupils must become aware that we often read painstakingly, only to reject the whole work because it is useless to our purpose.

The main task of synthesis here, therefore, is to join two very complex and abstract generalizations: one a forbidding paradox about the future, the other a climactic summary of the past. The basic outlook of each seems to negate that of the other; yet a joining is possible on a higher abstraction—the pervasive spread of technology. Unless we care to revel in mere personal opinion, the pupils must be taught to seek the strategy of joining these two second-level abstractions. The pupils must see that to exclude or negate is a form of relation; to reveal or prove that two ideas or elements cannot be joined within a certain context is as important as to prove that they can be. In every joining there is an excluding, sometimes more being excluded than joined. One cannot join the totality of one passage with the totality of another passage; if so, the passages would be identical, or exclusive. Understanding this, of course, is a discovery too. Yet even if identical, there would probably be a difference in space; or, for instance, if the passages were two Temple oranges, probably a difference in weight, or, perhaps, too, in sugar content. We may want to grade them by size (a form of relation); or for a better strain, by the chemistry of the juice (another form of relation).

The key to good teaching of thinking through reading is that the teacher be aware of the mode of thinking he is entering when he is preparing to teach a passage or work: 1) what strategies of thought it takes to sustain the logical process, to move it along; and 2) how it may come to reasonable pedagogical completion. I say pedagogical because there is never complete comprehension in reading, even by scholars. The key to excellent teaching of reading is to foster in the pupils a sensitivity to the operations that are the logical process rather than to the finality of the relation.

Relating two poems. We have illustrated the logic of synthesis in reading with two short prose passages. Bringing together two poems provides a further challenge to the logic of synthesis, because with poetry we have not only ideas to relate but also tone and personal reactions.

Since children of junior high school age love animals, "Four Little Foxes" should of itself engender considerable excitement for such readers.

FOUR LITTLE FOXES

Speak gentle, Spring, and make no sudden sound;
For in my windy valley, yesterday I found
Newborn foxes squirming on the ground—
    Speak gently.

Walk softly, March, forbear the bitter blow;
Her feet within a trap, her blood upon the snow,
The four little foxes saw their mother go—
    Walk softly.

Go lightly, Spring, oh, give them no alarm;
When I covered them with boughs to shelter them from harm
The thin blue foxes suckled at my arm—
    Go lightly.

Step softly, March, with your rampant hurricane;
Nuzzling one another, and whimpering with pain,
The new little foxes are shivering in the rain—
    Step softly.

— Lew Sarett

The pupils should be allowed to share with one another their past experiences with young chicks, young birds, tadpoles, puppies, babies. What is there about being newly born that thrills us? Perhaps the trusting innocence, the helplessness, the fresh beauty, the playfulness. The newborn all need our care. Does nature always care for its own young? How? What kind of person is speaking? What is the tone of his voice? How do we detect that tone? How and why does the speaker repeat himself? Is there a singing quality about it? Will Spring listen? Why doesn't the speaker instead beg trappers and hunters in the same way? What line in the poem stands out as particularly appealing to us? Did you ever have a young animal lick your skin as if to beg for food or show its liking for you? What is nice about the word *nuzzle*? Why do we respond kindly to whimpering? The teacher may wish to digress widely but lightly from the poem at this stage by opening up or pursuing a discussion on how men and animals share the earth together, the decline of animal life as technology and industry advance. So far we are analyzing, encouraging at the same time an encounter with the poem. This kind of analysis is what we would hope any sensitive teacher would do within a single literary work.

Now that we have endeavored to engage the pupils in the poem and to explore the poem a bit rhetorically, let us analyze it further for its meaning. Actually, a good encounter, the pupils' empathy with the condition of the young foxes, is itself the meaning of the lyric; but the pupils should perceive how each stanza progressively adds some thought or image, and how each joins with the others to create the feeling and tone; how each stanza, though different in what it says, has a prayer-like utterance in common with the others. (Notice how we are using the logical operators *and* and *or*. Each stanza is an invocation, with a different given reason for the renewal of each plea. The sing-song repetition accumulates incrementally into a general feeling. Suppose the begging were limited to one stanza. The implication of the joining in stanza two is that man, in this case, instigated this pitiful predicament. Why does the speaker, who surely knows that nature does not hear, beg Spring to be gentle this year? Why March? In the poem itself is there any indication that either man or Spring will care for these helpless creatures? Is the speaker talking to Spring or to us, hoping we will overhear? What do you feel, now that you have overheard? Notice that the questions are such that cognitive analysis leads to feeling and feeling prompts more understanding. The poetry creates the frustration of sheer hopelessness.

The second poem, Frost's "The Pasture," continues the sense of wonder and awe about "newness."

THE PASTURE

I'm going out to clean the pasture spring;
I'll only stop to rake the leaves away
(And wait to watch the water clear, I may):
I shan't be gone long.—You come too.

I'm going out to fetch the little calf
That's standing by the mother. It's so young
It totters when she licks it with her tongue.
I shan't be gone long.—You come too.

— Robert Frost

The participation in renewal is presented here as the purity of a clearing spring and as seeing the fresh wobbly calf. Such delightful pictures usually come upon us with surprise as we work and go about our daily lives. Other pictures might be brought up in class with this kind of question: Do you have little pictures in your mind like these in the poem—lovely experiences you maybe invited somebody to share with you? Perhaps something like these will emerge from the class—a little bird trying its wings, a light-breaking bud of a wild flower under a leaf, a moth coming out of a chrysalis, the clear blue of a baby brother's eyes, a lost kitten behind a garbage can. The lyric returns the pupils to experience.

In this lyric, much more than in "Four Little Foxes," feeling and meaning tend to fuse. As in the first poem there is a progression of thought from stanza to stanza—at first sight, the joining of two images or episodes—but it is also the union of two memorable experiences: of two newly-fresh, pure, sensory delights and of an invitation to participate in them. We might ask what phrases explicitly are joined, and what quality in the two images permits the joining. More concretely, what do the images "to watch the water clear" and "It totters when she licks it ... " have in common when one is inanimate and the other is animate? Why would the speaker assume that anyone would want to come along? The teacher will find that the pupils will be darting intuitively and randomly from this poem to the other, despite his attempt to control the analysis of this one. This is all to the good. For the approaching synthesis will bring the two lyrics into a focus.

Joining as a logical process

After the class has analyzed the two poems separately, the act of synthesizing can then be taught. First, ask the pupils if one poem is related to the other in any way—a deliberately wide-open question that probes for a focus. There will be a wide range of replies—some trivial, some wildly illogical. This is done to let the pupils settle upon a purpose that would generate comparison. Is there something in one that helps us understand the other; or, having read both, do we come to some new thought or point not in either? If no seminal ideas spring out of the group, the teacher may ask: How did you feel while you were reading the first poem? What seemed to stir up that feeling? What was your feeling like in the second poem? If you had different feelings, where, however, were they alike? Or are they entirely different? Are the two speakers talking in the same way or tone? One invites; the other pleads or begs. Why? In comparing two poems, the pupils should gradually realize that joining entails a bringing together of certain ideas and an exclusion of other ideas.

Several kinds of possible joinings we hope the pupils will advance are 1) both are about animals just born, 2) both are about nature, 3) both depict human response. These abstractions, the teacher must realize, are not going very deeply into the poems. And merely listing a number of likenesses and a number of differences is not a comparison that effects a synthesis. Therefore, the teacher may now suggest this operation: We might invent a point of view or a focus, some third idea, some reason for joining. Could we think of and name several such purposes? From a free-for-all discussion, these general ideas for joining the two may inductively issue forth: 1) the beauty of newly-born life, 2) the feelings that the newborn arouse in us, 3) the fate of wild animals and of farm animals, 4) the two speakers sharing their concern with others, 5) man and animals living together. Perhaps some pupil may make a case for a separation (disjunction)—that is, survival of wild and of domestic animals. Let him defend it.

At a higher level of abstraction, some pupils may care to speak or write on A) tenderness and beauty within hopelessness and B) tenderness and beauty within delight. What a strange contrast in "Step softly" and "You come too." Are they disjunctive? The teacher might ask the students to write a paragraph using one or more of these purposes to join ideas in both the poems, or he might ask them to jot down some notes for a little talk on one of these ways of joining the two poems, using support from both. He might discuss with the pupils our former diagram, urging them to pick as their purpose one of the possibilities for focus presented in class.

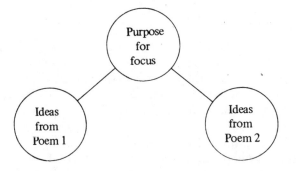

Afterwards, the teacher may have the various joinings read in class to see how they differ from one another and how they are alike. This kind of discussion becomes an adventure in logic. He can see, too, whether someone in class had a way of joining unlike any already suggested by the class. Reading their own offerings is, of course, a way for students to learn to read better, for reading the poems becomes after that a check on the relation of their writing to their thought. In this way, we are training the pupils that a stance, a purpose, is necessary for good comparing. "Just comparing" gets us nowhere. In his *Logic of Scientific Discovery,* Karl P. Popper (1959) states the idea in this way: " . . . that things may be similar in *different respects,* and that any two things which are from one point of view similar may be dissimilar from another point of view." (p. 421)

Despite our stress on thinking in relating these two lyrics, we were trying very much to stay within the affective domain: the pupil's state of mind sustains the strategy of the logical quest; thus the state of mind of one pupil is itself open to the state of mind of others in the class. The pupils can compare their different responses and the probable reasons they do differ. In doing this, pupils are analyzing (separating out) their various syntheses.

Comparison as a form of joining. Comparison, a subcategory of joining, can be used often in reading to develop a concept. We must remember that the child was comparing freely in an intuitive way before he entered school and before he could read, and he will continue to do it, in most circumstances, for the rest of his life outside reading and outside school. Piaget (1957) writes, "The adolescent is not conscious of the system of propositional operations. He undoubtedly uses these operations, but he does this without enumerating them or reflecting on them or their relationships, and he only faintly suspects that they form such a system. He is unaware of this, in the same way that in singing or whistling he is unaware of the laws of harmony." (pp. 39-40) Our reading problem, therefore, is to teach him the strategies of comparison in terms of written or printed words put in sentences, paragraphs, chapters, and certain patterns called literary forms.

Because teachers observe this intuitive force at work in pupils, many take for granted that pupils can already perform well the strategies that compose the complete act of comparison. I have never observed a teacher discuss with pupils what one does when one compares, for few teachers understand the logic of comparison. But just as syntax (which children already use unconsciously before they enter school) must be made explicit gradually in the course of language development, so the grammar of comparison must in time be made explicit if it is to be refined. The pedagogical problem is to have the pupil become conscious of the strategies of comparison so that he may improve this form of joining within written and printed materials, thereby improving his reading. Comparison as a form of joining for a certain purpose must therefore be taught. Let us thus study the strategies of comparison and then afterwards apply them to the teaching of reading.

First of all, theoretically, what strategies do we want the pupil eventually to possess when he compares on his own? The pupil should come to see that comparison is possible only within the larger relation of joining. No two things in the universe, he should begin to realize, are intrinsically alike except in connection with a particular purpose for looking. The pupil must learn that all overlap of apparently disparate things is proximate, that overlap always springs from a point of view, that the differences in things outside their overlap may be crucial and irreconcilable yet at the same time, strangely, sustain the overlap. Even very bright pupils must be taught to come to understand that similarity is possible because of differences—that accepting an element as similar means rejecting another as extraneous to the evolving web of similarity, but that the third element is necessary to each of the objects because it makes the elements of likeness possible. For example, the plays *Macbeth* and *Hamlet* are totally unlike yet can be compared in respect to tragedy. The logical task would be to detect, prove, and accept certain tragic elements (our definition of tragedy) in each despite the vast dissimilarity between the two plots and the two heroes. Macbeth is obsessed with over-vaulting ambition while Hamlet is seemingly genetically passive; yet these antithetical characters can be compared in respect to our definition of tragedy. Reading for comparison demands a rigorous selection of one idea rather than another among many ideas. The resulting concept will be clearer and more accurate than any prepared definition of the concept. Vygotsky (1962) goes so far as to maintain that a teacher cannot give a pupil a concept—that the pupil must earn it. The logic of comparison is one of several ways of earning a concept.

To repeat, comparison allows us to bring things together that we think need to be together, despite conspicuous differences. For this strategy in language we have the conjunction *and* and connectives such as *furthermore* and *moreover* as well as figures of speech such as the *simile* and the *metaphor*.

The overlap by which we are able to join or group things at all is an idea, a principle, a class, a generalization, a situation, a set of criteria. Pears and apples may be brought together for all kinds of purposes: because they are fruit or are at hand in the refrigerator or are a choice for dinner or are a display at the market. Yet as fruit they are distinctly different in taste and in shape, in skin texture, and in the chemical makeup of the juice. Pears and bricks, which seem very far apart by nature, may be joined as objects thrown at someone or as stolen. Actually, the relating of two things in terms of their similarities—whether they be events, objects, poems, or stories—requires a closer scrutiny of each than if it were only being examined singly by act of analysis. In fact, we often fail to understand a thing—a poem, a story, or an episode—until we try to join it (compare it) to another poem, story, or episode by noting the fit or the overlap. Even when we assume we are reading a poem or passage or paragraph analytically for itself alone in order to see what it is, we are bringing some past experience, some assimilated performance, some familiarity, with us to the task, consciously or unconsciously. A reader cannot will his past experience to bear on a work, but he can train himself to forge a context whenever he intends to compare. Some reading specialists call this act of relating experience or background or present events to a reading a *skill*. Actually, this deliberate search for a context, is a learned habit of mind, and it need not be taught as a skill so long as the pupil grows more and more aware of a purpose in reading; for then he will be impelled to bring from outside the work something to bear on what he is reading. Purpose thus establishes a context for reading, and for this reason is part of the logical process of comparison.

Comparison as a logical process. In set theory, the graph for the act of joining, which incorporates comparison, assumes this form:

$$x = (A - a) + (B - b)$$
$$A = a + x$$
$$B = b + x$$
C = the context in which A and B exist
D = the domain that sets limits to the context

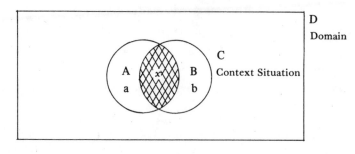

The symbol x indicates the reason why the likenesses, the two things or ideas (A and B) may be joined; a is something stubborn or resistant or contrasting within A that cannot go into x and must lie outside the joining (x), yet it is something that is peculiar and necessary to A. The same is true of b to B. Though a of A and b of B singly are utterly unlike each other, *together* they are removed (excluded) from x. To be able to explain why this is so is the essence of what we call comprehension. Out of two different entities, so to speak, arises likeness. This is possible because of the context C. The domain D may, and usually does, influence C. A change of purpose

(*C*) changes the nature of *x*; as purpose (*C*) changes, some of *a* and some of *b* get into *x* and some of *x* back into *a* and *b*. It is the obligation of a good reader to explain how this takes place.

Comparison as an act of joining is also inherent in the act of making the common figures of speech like simile and metaphor—for example, "John is a fox." Some person does not know how John deals with people when at business. He does not know what John is like in this respect (this context of business). People do know, it is assumed, that the chief characteristic of a fox is its slyness. There-fore, we cross over, carry over, (the literal meaning of *metaphor*) from John to fox; that is, we move from *A* (John) to *B* (fox) because they have something in common—slyness (x)—in the context *business*, although both John and a fox are very different in most ways and John may not behave slyly at home. Our main purpose for creating the metaphor is to inform how John behaves when he is handling a business deal. This need for communicating about John is the domain (*D*). Actually, this is the way figures of speech should be taught, not in themselves, merely to be identified.

In sum, comparison, as one relation called joining, can be de-scribed specifically by these behaviors:

1) Explaining why—in the name of what—two unlike things may be joined—their likenesses (*x*).

2) Showing the nature of *A*. How much of it will go into *x*.

3) Showing the nature of *B*. How much of it will go into *x*.

4) Revealing the peculiar exclusion (negation) of both *a* and *b* from the principle of joining.

5) Describing the context or situation that allows the joining or occasions the joining.

When such strategies are delineated in this unified way, we use the term *task model.* In this case, we have described the complete task of comparison in five steps. The teacher should be aware of the strategies in the model so that he can guide the pupil in reading for comparison. The pupil should be taught to use the strategies of the model and, in part, his progress in reading should be measured by observing how he handles the strategies while comparing two pas-sages or works.

With two things he knows well, the pupil will go through these five strategies of comparison in lightning fashion with all coalescing intuitively. But in fresh encounters, he may never join expertly un-less he is taught. More and more cursory reading or wide reading will not generally increase his skill in this kind of reading for synthesis if he relies only on experience. Other potential and more significant likenesses for joining may escape him or be utterly unknown to him, despite wide experience. For example, unless he is immersed in chemistry or biology, his knowledge of apples and pears will be practical but most likely superficial, thus limiting his skill in joining the two. He would need to distinguish between their seeds, the character of their leaves, and the specific form and arrangement of their blossoms—distinctions which lie removed from the two as palpable fruits. So it is with reading for relation. The pupil can be delivered from mere practical, cursory reading when he is asked to create a relation. For example, he may be asked to discover the relation between a good story which is well-nigh plotless and another one that is also good yet nearly all plot. The nature of the commonness of quality in them would then have to be explored: goodness is our x bridging the stories; yet both stories are antithetical in technique as well as in theme.

Over the school years, part of the reading curriculum for youth should be one of running through the declension of comparison among literary forms—the variations amid the same form and the strategic differences among the forms. One of the most basic logical processes in reading literary works is that of relating content and form, while abstracting one from the other—"the different forms that may be exhibited by the same material . . . the same form [that] may be exemplified by different contents." (Langer, 1953, pp. 26-27) The Portland, Oregon, curriculum (1965) is built around this process of logic. The junior high school curriculum is held together by having the pupils read a work examining three aspects—subject, form, and point of view. The creators of this curriculum state the logic of this kind of reading in this way: "Subject and form have the great virtue of reciprocality; we can ask, 'Why this form for this subject?' or 'Why this subject for this form?' . . . an attempted or artificial separation can illuminate the work as totality . . . ." (pp. 4-11) Just as it is a great advance in the act of joining when the pupil sees that the difference between a pear and an orange lies not in looking at the outward fruit at all but probably elsewhere in leaf, blossom, or the chemistry of the juice—so in reading, the pupil's skill in joining is greatly sharpened when he realizes that another literary work must be explored if he wishes to trace fully the recesses of the work before him.

Purpose as a strategy in comparison. Yet we teachers must ever be aware that there is no comparison in life for its own sake and that we will provide very little chance for growth in thinking if we continually set tasks—such as "Compare these two stories, these two poems, these two quotations"—merely as a school exercise. In such cases, we ask pupils to compare for the classroom's or the teacher's sake, and neither is a good reason for initiating a logical quest. Comparison is invoked in order to find out something in terms of a larger mission. "Invention," writes Blanshard (1955), "is purpose assuming authority over the course of ideas." (p. 128) An assignment that invites comparison for its own sake cannot develop a concept, for all we get is a column of likenesses and a column of differences, a boxful of *L*'s, a boxful of *D*'s—and to what end? Actually, this kind of summary-by-listing should never be begun unless we intend to use the items to some logical purpose clear to the pupils. Having a purpose does not, however, tolerate mere listings of details separated-out, because purpose rejects and discards similarities and differences not pertinent to the quest. For example, Fred Hechinger, writing in the education section of the *New York Times* (January 17, 1971), adopted a brilliant logical strategy to describe Durek Bok, Harvard's new president. He could have given a character sketch of the man, listed his qualities, and organized his background. He could have given this sort of vita and have stopped there. But he chose instead to go outside the character delineation itself to Kingman Brewster, Yale's president; to reveal the similarities of the two men; and then to contrast these two with Nathan Pusey and James K. Conant, two former Harvard presidents. By using this strategy of comparison followed by contrast, he not only explained the nature of Bok (which his descriptive vita might have done), but he also placed before us an academic situation in the United States, stressing how the times and recent events are creating a demand for a new kind of university president—not a classicist, not a scientist, but a negotiator. Hechinger's purpose led him to perform two comparisons and finally a contrast between the two sets of comparisons.

Context as a strategy in comparison. There can be no thinking without a direction. Pupils must come to recognize the need for both context and purpose in reading. They should know the reason they are trying to join or separate. Years ago in teaching Shakespeare, assignments such as "compare Gertrude and Ophelia" and "contrast Hamlet and Laertes" were handed out arbitrarily. Such classroom assignments led to dead-end thinking, for the comparisons were without a context, and the context without a focus. One person's comparison is another person's contrast. One kind of purpose searches for certain items; another purpose turns up other items of likeness. By asking such questions outside a context, a teacher can procure from a pupil only a list of recalled particulars put up in aimless juxtaposition. Broudy (1961), in writing on the mastery of concepts comes to this conclusion, "When, therefore, we speak of mastery in the sense that knowing something is to master it, we mean an awareness of an appropriate context that grounds the adaptive response . . . ." (p. 82)

Selection: contrast as separation and exclusion

The common sense meaning of *contrast* is to accentuate striking differences and let it go at that. In aesthetics, it is a source of delight. But why, logically, is a difference striking? Only when we have expected a similarity or are faced with a baffling choice in an *or* disjunction. Contrast as an operation is not the creation of two columns of several polar differences drawn up in a one-to-one paired relation. Reading teachers often have pupils do this. Actually, a contrast is an emphasis within a context (what and why one wants to, or must, contrast at all); and so contrast always literally involves noting similarities as well. That is, the task of contrast is to reveal how difficult it is to determine x in our model, where x means to establish some kind of base or to support vast similarities. To handle this task in language we have the syntactic forms of *but—despite, however, although*—and figures of speech like *antithesis, irony,* and *paradox.* The operation called disjunction (separating)—that which cannot be joined because only one of two can be selected—lies within the common sense meaning of contrast.

Contrast as a relation. Operationally, then, logical contrast means that *A* and *B* are so exclusive, so "either . . . or" in nature, that reconciliation is arduous; we are driven to search for commonality though none seems within the cases before us. Therefore, the pupil should be taught, as the strategy proceeds, that contrast, like comparison, is not done just for the sake of it, but always for a reason. Because the contrast may violate one's expectations, the cognitive challenge is very dramatic and often soul shaking; and when the two ideas involved are deeply rooted in us and have long lain unresolved, the task may frustrate us. The cognitive conflict thus involves the affective domain. In Herbart's (1806) association psychology, the conflict of ideas is the source of emotion. It seems strange that elementary and secondary language arts, as well as most reading instruction, are both devoid of giving pupils practice in the strategy of reconciling contrasts or opposites, as if we want to spare pupils this kind of thinking. Yet as pupils grow, they constantly and inevitably encounter these conflicts, which are, operationally, logical contrasts that tend to move into an *or* situation. In fact, healthful human growth depends on logically facing such resolutions as we move through time.

The teacher can set up some contrasts that are so very exciting that the *either . . . or* inherently sets up its own motivation. Diedrich

(1955) in his beautifully designed exercises in critical thinking worked out this situation (Number 15, pp. 199-207) juxtaposing the following two passages from the Bible:

Go to the ant, thou sluggard:
Consider her ways, and be wise:
Which, having no chief,
Overseer, or ruler,
Provideth her meat in the summer,
And gathereth her food in the harvest.

How long wilt thou sleep, O sluggard?
When wilt thou arise out of thy sleep?
Yet a little sleep, a little slumber,
A little folding of the hands to sleep:
So shall thy poverty come as a robber,
And thy want as an armed man.

— Old Testament

A PARABLE BY JESUS

And why take ye thought for raiment? Consider the lilies of the field, how they grow; they toil not, neither do they spin: and yet I say unto you that even Solomon in all his glory was not arrayed like one of these.

Wherefore, if God so clothe the grass of the field, which today is, and tomorrow is cast into the oven, shall he not much more clothe you, O ye of little faith?

Therefore take no thought, saying, what shall we eat? or, What shall we drink? or, Wherewithal shall we be clothed? For after all these things do the Gentiles seek; for your heavenly Father knoweth that ye have need of all these things. But seek ye first the kingdom of God and his righteousness; and all these things shall be added unto you.

Take therefore no thought for the morrow, for the morrow shall take thought for the things of itself. Sufficient unto the day is the evil thereof.

— New Testament

Diedrich sets up the problem so informally and graciously that I quote him:

... explain the seeming contradiction between the two passages, both from the Bible. First explain what the apparent contradiction is, and show the dilemma in which a devout believer is placed. Then write a careful explanation of what you understand the two passages to mean, supporting your interpretation with relevant quotations. Examine the case for the "ant" then the case for the "lilies," giving reasons for acting in accordance with each position and showing what difficulties and losses an extreme adherence to either position would entail. Finally, try to work out a resolution of the conflict: either a way of reconciling the two passages or some ground between them that you would regard as a tenable position. (p. 199)

The next day, after a number of pupils have read their tenable positions, the class usually breaks out into a spirited discussion. The motivation is intrinsic; there need be no contrived relevance. After this warm-up, Diedrich presents a still more knotty problem issuing from three philosophical positions. He brings together a passage from Thoreau on progress, a section on fate from the *Rubaiyat,* and the parable on faith just cited. He addresses the students,

> ... the first questions in this reading exercise require you to perceive what problem all three passages have in common and how they differ in approaches and solutions. (p. 199)

Notice that he conceives this entire approach as a reading exercise. I know of no reading texts or language arts texts of any of the book companies that arrange readings so as to develop nice strategies of thought, except here and there a light gesture toward such loose directives as "discuss," "compare," "think over," "ponder the work," "what about," "what do you think." Sometimes there is a mix of works around a catch-all theme, but there is little or no planned internal development suggested by an interplay of the strategies of analysis and synthesis.

In a former discussion of pedagogical order, we warned that the move from engagement to synthesis, bypassing analysis, was hazardous. But the reverse is likely to increase motivation because an attempted synthesis of a dramatic conflict (an *or* situation) sometimes instigates a renewed engagement with the work. The excitement of the quest for synthesis, it seems, will motivate the pupils to a rigorous rereading (analysis) of each passage.

I have seen pupils in my sophomore classes cry out as if in pain by a rude contrast; others often just sit awhile, confounded, in awe; others are indignant that they are reminded of what evidently had plagued them a long while—their unresolved thoughts long stuffed away in them by English-as-coverage. Logical contrast, let me reiterate, is not a mere intellectualization of poetry: the search for reconciliation can go deeply into self.

A textbook that comes close to what we are describing here as *reading for concept development* by comparison and contrast is *The World of Poetry* (1965) by Rockowitz and Kaplan, where at the end of each unit or theme, there are questions endeavoring to pull various views together by having the pupil examine the poems in groups of three's or four's, putting at times two poems against two others; but all these joinings and separations, unfortunately, do not guide the pupils toward the creation of a generalization (synthesis). In respect to logical process, the weakness in this text is that the questions are such as to bail the pupils out of the indeterminate situation they set up, and so do not attempt to make the pupils aware of the strategy of thought necessary for the task. The strength of the editing lies, however, in an ingenious juxtaposition (contrast) of poems to evoke a train of thought toward conceptualization. For instance, in one section they set up a contrast between hedonism and stoicism. At the end of every section, as in the one on "Nature as Teacher," comprising 15 poems, there are unit questions that guide the students toward a conceptualization of the theme by encouraging comparison and contrast of groups of poems. (p. 435) A key question, as good as it is as an organizer of subjective response, is not, of course, our concept development. It results in little synthesis or interpretation by the students of the similarities and differences among the poems at ever higher abstract levels. But the procedure could be made so by a teacher aware of logical process in teaching.

Separation: discriminating differences. Sometimes a contrast assumes the form of essential difference, and we have a completely separating operation. Confectionary sugar and arsenic look alike, but the appearance is superficial, not essential; one is a food, the other a poison. Chemically, they are so contrasting as to be only a mixture if physically joined; mixing does not create a reaction between the two.

What sometimes starts out to be a search for contrast may end in a discovered deviation from an ethical norm or a need to probe for the most fundamental difference. The more two things, beliefs, or literary works become alike, the more the need to delineate any real cleavage. For example, at present in the Western world there is a growing ecumenical (joining) movement among religions, based largely on the surprising discovery of much similarity between Catholicism and Protestantism. Out of this new condition, there is a concomitant need to probe for the most outstanding difference—the most basic factor in, or cause of, the present separation.

At an early age pupils should be taught 1) how to read for the rock-bottom uniqueness of a concept, which can only be found by a series of attempted joinings that fail; and 2) how to read when confronted by two concepts that seem impossible to be joined. The logic of separation thus becomes crucial during the act of choice.

Separation: the logic of choice. Sometimes there are situations in the real world where continued delineation and a continued probing for commonality seem impossible. This kind of dichotomy is not subject to a logical synthesis. It is an *or* situation; here the two elements or works lie side by side, and the only recourse is to judge and value each and then to choose one according to our end in view.

This is what we do at election time: we must select only one, not both. There is some good and bad in each candidate, so what is the basis for a decision? Even not to vote is a choice! In reading, the logic of the task resides in such questions as these: Which poem is a lyric (both maybe)? Is this play a tragedy? Which story is contrived? Which story better interprets technology? Which of the two depicts adolescence the better? Such separation generally compels evaluation. Seldom do our anthologies and workbooks provide pupils with much opportunity to practice the logic of disjunction (selecting).

This whole section under the topic of contrast represents the place of logical difference in thinking. Such operations as separation, exclusion, conflict, discrimination, choice, arise in our daily acts and in our daily reading. The pupil should be so trained in reading that he perceives separation in one sense as a strategy toward synthesis (ripping off all accretions until the pattern is clear) or a strategy toward the most rational or artistic or expedient or normative choice. Pupils should be trained in reading to make certain kinds of choices among literary works from all these stances; and to distinguish among these choices, too, as he encounters them in his reading.

Structure as process

The strategy of extension. So far we have been studying how the four operators intuitively work to establish a relation or a joining or to lead to a nonjoining (disjunction or separation), which is a positive contribution. Also, we have explained (analyzed) how the acts of comparison and contrast enter into the process of synthesis.

But whatever conceptual synthesis we appropriately create for a given situation is always openended, tentative, unstable, imperfect to some degree. To let the resulting joining or separation rest as if fulfilled, to infer that the concept at this stage is now clear and accurate, as if finished, and to give the pupils the view that the resulting relation is now *known* is to belie the nature of conceptualization and to betray the pupils both logically and pedagogically. The following statement, although it seems true, is typical of the failure in teaching reading as concept development: "One of the important responsibilities of a teacher at any school level is to further the growth of clear and accurate concepts which can be used in reading or any other activity." (Sochor, 1959)

Concepts are not first made clear and accurate in order to be used later on in reading; they cannot be made clear and accurate in themselves—in a definition or a dictionary or a vocabulary drill— divorced from a progressive development of the concept. Concepts are not coins of a certain stated denomination constant throughout an exchange. They are made clear and accurate through reading and doing art and science, particularly by reading literature, by continually performing throughout our school days certain operations on and with language.

Since all concepts are evolving, are never completely clear, are never accurately used even by scholars, and are always psychologically assimilated as well as logically held, a difficult problem in teaching reading as concept development is that once a relation has been formed, the pupils should come to perceive what strategies are needed to develop it. A concept freshly attained—a generalization, a comparison, a joining—still needs to be put to logical use. This is not a mere application of something now known but becomes a further growth in meaning. The most stable concepts and facts change in use—a watt, a dollar, tragedy, Waterloo, distance—as we use them in literal experience or the experience of ideas. The first stage in development is the strategy of extension.

The moving out of the generalization (the newly-formed concept) to ingest other elements or entities is what we call *extension.* In reading, a concept is made more clear when a student is taught the strategy of seeking what is common among more literary works or passages than those he has just read, and yet at the same time is able to delineate the uniqueness that justifies the existence or completeness of each literary work. In this process, the generalization is modified (becomes more accurate) as more and more entities are sought for and then brought under it. Other entities, during the process, once entertained as a possibility, are rejected and put somewhere else—either put into another kind of generalization or deliberately left dangling. Rejecting a case also contributes to the sharpening of the generalization. The key pedagogical words here are *sought for* (the pupil must be searching on his own). Equally vital is the *use* of the concept—not statically as in a sentence, a paragraph, or a composition, but actively to find out how appropriate the concept is to a new situation or how inadequate it is in another. Extension is a mode of testing the limits of the concept. Definitions are only provisionally clear and accurate, even those made by literary critics and authorities in science. The pupil must, therefore, receive practice in using the concept in a variety of literary works.

Extension in concept development, then, has a two-dimensional aspect: 1) an analytical examination of each of several entities for the purpose of framing a generalization—which is an inductive movement; 2) the testing of this generalization, tentatively held, on other entities to determine whether they fit and/or change it—which is a deductive movement. The latter movement is the extensional aspect of concept development.

Teaching reading as concept development

Let us take two poems to show the two-dimensional strategy of extension in teaching reading. One is Ben Jonson's "The Noble Nature" and the other, Emerson's "The Mountain and the Squirrel." To begin, suppose we ask pupils to read the following poem. A study of the poem would first need some motivational setting (a context) to foster engagement.

The Mountain and The Squirrel

The mountain and the squirrel
Had a quarrel,
And the former called the latter "Little prig";
Bun replied,
"You are doubtless very big;
But all sorts of things and weather
Must be taken in together
To make up a year,
And a sphere,
And I think it no disgrace
To occupy my place.
If I'm not so large as you,
You are not so small as I,
And not half so spry;
I'll deny you make
A very pretty squirrel track.
Talents differ; all is well and wisely put;
If I cannot carry forests on my back,
Neither can you crack a nut."

— Ralph Waldo Emerson

To get at the internal relationship of the ideas in the poem, the conventional analytical teaching of reading would seek responses from such questions as these:

1. What two objects, ideas, and points are being related?
2. For what purpose are they being related?
3. What one line best brings out the meaning of the poem?
4. What is the key idea or meaning of the poem?

Sometimes, such questions are turned into more concrete, true-false statements or multiple-choice questions, such as:

1. What two things are being compared? (Circle two)

   a. a forest   d. a squirrel
   b. a mountain   e. a sphere
   c. a nut

2. True or False

   a. The author is trying to give the small guy in this world his due.
   b. The chief talent of the squirrel is his spryness.

These devices are supposedly used to test the pupil's comprehension, to foster his ability to think through the poem. Perhaps, too, such concrete informational questions as these are proposed:

1. What two things are being compared?
2. What can the squirrel do?
3. What can the mountain do?
4. What can one do that the other cannot?

Usually, after this kind of testing and questioning, the reading is finished and the teacher turns to another work and does practically the same thing over again in teaching another poem. The foregoing pedagogical treatment does not foster concept development.

If the teacher is pedagogically aware of teaching thinking, these higher level questions will be worked in as well:

1. Can one kind of talent be said to be better than another?
2. Why is the size of the two compared?
3. Does the squirrel need the mountain? The mountain need the squirrel?
4. Can anything exist alone—a stone, a human being?

In contrast to such approaches, our analytical method would trace how the logic of the comparison proceeds toward creating a set of internal relations. Fundamentally, there is a negation here: size bears no relation to talent, for talent is its own worth; different kinds of talent cannot be compared. Why? What in the poem is the common ground (x) to support this negation? Could it be that all talent depends for its existence on other talents? Does (x) imply a philosophy of life? The ultimate question would be: Does this view of talent apply only to nature? Under what circumstances does it apply to society too? Between a laborer and an executive? In short, how far can this view be extended? At this stage, suppose now that we present the pupils with the second poem, asking them to keep in mind the view expressed in the first poem.

The Noble Nature

It is not growing like a tree
In bulk, doth make man better be;
Or standing long an oak three hundred year,
To fall a log at last, dry, bald, and sere;
    A lily of a day
    Is fairer far in May,
Although it fall and die that night—
It was the plant and flower of Light.
In small proportions we just beauty see;
And in short measures life may perfect be.

— Ben Jonson

Again, conventional reading techniques would ask questions of this sort to guide and measure comprehension of this particular poem:

1. What is the key idea or meaning of the poem?
2. What one line best brings out the meaning of the poem?
3. What objects, ideas, and points are being related?
4. For what purpose are they being related?

This kind of questioning often goes on for a dozen poems or passages, day after day, several a day, all on different themes and by as many different authors. With this method, of course, the deepest comprehension of each may not be attained because there is little, if any, interrelatedness in the reading, either in respect to refining a logical process or forming and developing a concept. This kind of successive reading piles up—as Bruner puts it— "information drift." Granted that the reader might improve his ability to draw out the literal meaning of each and perhaps be able to think somewhat better, still there is no indication of how this "better thinking" would be ascertained. This method of questioning would hardly be said to foster abstract reasoning, because no concepts are being developed, and certainly none are becoming more clear and accurate—that is, extended.

As a foil to the first poem, this second poem, pedagogically speaking, was selected with great care and has almost the same internal logical relation as the first— a negation. Beauty is not related to duration.

Two generalizations, each in the form of a negation, now confront the reader: 1) the worth of talent is not related to the size of the skill; 2) the quality of beauty is not related to its duration. How are they to be put together? Is the following an adequate third level abstraction or only a summary: talent and beauty do not depend upon size or duration? Is it fair to say that talent does not depend upon duration; that beauty does not depend upon size? Even if both are true, do the internal relations of each poem warrant this synthesizing abstraction? Duration is certainly implied in poem one but not made explicit, and size is certainly implied in poem two but not made explicit. Another try at synthesis would go something like this: Size and duration are material attributes while talent and beauty are spiritual qualities; therefore, the intrinsic worth of spiritual qualities does not directly relate to their physical existence.

Let us draw up a rather formidable-looking diagram to try plotting the movements of the four operators as the mind endeavors to synthesize the two poems (see figure).

I. MOVEMENT TOWARD ABSTRACTION

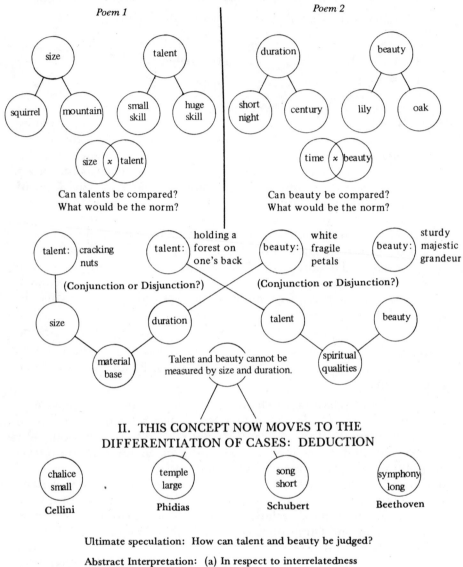

Poem 1

Poem 2

size — squirrel, mountain

talent — small skill, huge skill

duration — short night, century

beauty — lily, oak

size (x) talent

time (x) beauty

Can talents be compared?
What would be the norm?

Can beauty be compared?
What would be the norm?

talent: cracking nuts

talent: holding a forest on one's back

beauty: white fragile petals

beauty: sturdy majestic grandeur

(Conjunction or Disjunction?)

(Conjunction or Disjunction?)

size — duration — material base

talent — beauty — spiritual qualities

Talent and beauty cannot be measured by size and duration.

II. THIS CONCEPT NOW MOVES TO THE DIFFERENTIATION OF CASES: DEDUCTION

chalice small
Cellini

temple large
Phidias

song short
Schubert

symphony long
Beethoven

Ultimate speculation: How can talent and beauty be judged?

Abstract Interpretation: (a) In respect to interrelatedness
(b) In respect to continuous time

Once the generalization is proposed—in this case, either 1) beauty and talent cannot be measured by duration or size or 2) spiritual qualities do not depend upon the state of their existence—the movement of thought turns away from induction and spreads outward toward more cases, to test the range of the generalization. It now becomes deductive—hypothetical: If this generalization just made is warranted, it must be usable in other than the above poems. Can two poems create a universal? We now ask the pupils to think of talent of all kinds, small and large, not so much to see whether the generalization is workable, but to see to what extent it is workable. An example may arise: Tolstoy's giant *War and Peace* cannot be compared logically with Herrick's short-flighted lyrics. Both are needed; each has its place. Is *Vanity Fair* a greater work of art than *Dover Beach*? Are novels needed more than lyrics? Schubert's songs, as short as they are, have a kind of beauty not to be rivaled by a Beethoven symphony. How is Nathan Hale to be measured against George Washington? Yet, in sports there seems to be some relation between size and talent. Is winning the marathon more of a feat than winning the one hundred meter dash? Surely, too, some brief interval may hold more beauty for us than several months of living. People plan for days to recapture such a moment. By such an application, we engage the pupils in thinking upon their reading, which drives them back into a rereading. The cognitive may be transformed into the affective by pointing out for discussion that "human squirrels" ever strive to be mountains, and most people seemingly would rather be oaks than lilies!

Only when each poem is seen in its original context—its own contemporary philosophy—does the synthesis become of another kind. Both poems, too, were evoked by different occasions. Ultimately, we would have to reconcile Emerson's transcendentalism with Jonson's orthodox Christianity. Context thus makes us shift the questioning. Transcendentalism as a context prompts this inquiry, "Is this poem an aspect of transcendentalism or the all of it?" Is Jonson provoking us to think of interrelatedness, like Emerson, or something else? Does Jonson have the same reason for relating the lily and the oak as Emerson has for relating the squirrel to the mountain? Now read the Jonson poem as a response to a child's death. The lily is now a symbol. Is the squirrel serving as a symbol? Do the two poems have two different views of interrelatedness? How join them? Context, we see, charts a different course for reading to take.

On the grave of Ben Jonson in Westminster Abbey there is this epitaph,

> In small proportions we just beauty see:
> And in short measures life may perfect be.

The poems at this stage of joining can now be related not in themselves as poems but as illustrations of two different views of life—presumable, young death serves a purpose in the human condition just as the slight sinewy squirrel does in nature. Notice that as we proceed, we are growing a structure of thought at a still higher level of abstraction.

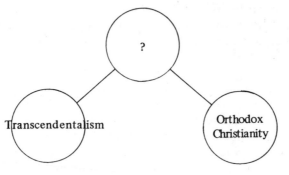

Good thinking is fostered through the kind of reading that prompts the reader to realize that a fuller comprehension of a text can be gained if he goes outside the immediate passage in order to relate it to another passage or to several recently read or to be read. This search implies a strategy wherein the student assigns the meaning of the present passage before him to a place in a tentative, constantly evolving structure of his own making and thereafter seeks its possible range and its levels of abstraction. By this strategy, a concept can be said to become more clear and accurate than it was before. The more the pupil extends the generalization, the clearer the concept becomes; he learns its tentative limits for the present, the part that cannot be included in it, and what part of it is still not known. When he reads in this way, whatever he writes or says can be said to be composed rather than merely put together.

A form of logical extension in teaching reading is the distance test. The pupil is asked to use the concept that he has created out of the literary materials of one kind of situation in coping with another situation not entirely made up of the same relations. Or he may be asked, as a way of testing how well a concept has become part of him, to extend it to another case or two not previously read at all. Reading tests of these kinds are forms of testing made integral to the teaching method, not as something scored afterward to see what has been comprehended. For in concept development, the pupil does not know and then behave. His behavior is a form of knowing. Since this kind of testing is for the most part a test of strategy, the final test is

sis. Yet if we prolong the process of extension, we produc
single-level concept of this kind:

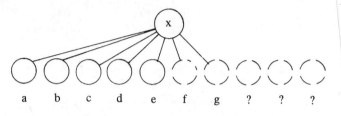

The concept is being developed as more cases or particulars a
under x. In other words, so long as the pupil continues to read
of a certain kind, capable of being subsumed under the crite
establish as x, the concept is growing in respect to those criteria
Eventually, there must be some kind of disposal of the accumu
assemblage of relations that extension provides. In most classr
in English, these relations are allowed to pile up in a miscellar
way throughout the year. Reading for concept development, t
fore, should teach the strategy of logically working with these
tions as they emerge from the extension of the concept. This m
that reading 20 novels may be no better than reading 10, for it
not necessarily produce a better conceptualization of the novel
genre. Under the proper kind of reading, the pupil can learn m
about tragedy from reading three Shakesperean plays than if he
read eight of them indiscriminately or than if he had read e;
carefully as an entity, line by line, in order to understand what v
going on in each play singly. For without the concept of tragedy
could never truly understand each play singly.

As the internal relations of a structure increase and tend to inte
twine, it is good for the pupil to survey the concept so far develope
as a system or structure of relations, as a totality with characteristi
different from any of its parts. If he does this kind of thinking, tw
things may happen. First, as the extension increases, the singl
dimension of the parts tends to break up into subcategories (lowe
level abstractions) if the pupil is exploring the structure as structure
second, more important to reading, the structure x may collide with
another complex structure y, which, for example, may be a number
of the new-type novels, (Vonnegut, for instance) which are also held
together by a common theory. A higher level of abstraction is then
required to unite the two structures of relations than the abstraction
that holds each individual structure together. Suppose structure y
were about as complex as x above; the teacher will sense the logical
nature of the task. For the union of two marbles or two trees is of
the same process as the union of two generalizations, except for the

level of abstraction, which at this stage involves more precision in phrasing and a keen analysis of each of the generalizations to be joined.

One way to help the pupil is to present the structures to him serially with progressive degrees of abstraction. For example,

Level 1   Level 2   Level 3

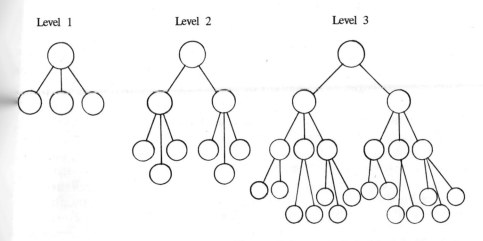

The semantic movement under Korzibsky and Hayakawa in the middle 1930s brought the teaching of abstraction into English classrooms; but these semanticists, although they rightfully warned the pupil against hollow abstractions—those without a referent or a denotation—underplayed the necessary and positive use of abstraction. Abstraction should be seen as the cement of a structure of ideas. As we pointed out before, specific concreteness is the worst possible way of joining complex ideas. For instance, the pupil is not synthesizing the two poems already discussed simply by saying, "The one is comparing a mountain and a squirrel and the other comparing a lily and an oak." Synthesis demands a joining of the two comparisons, and this task requires an abstraction higher than either. The greatest problem in the teaching of reading—of thinking itself, therefore—is how to join two high level generalizations. And this must be done if a concept is to be developed beyond the formative stage and the single-level relational stage of extension.

In sum, the second stage of concept development, then, is to build a structure of relations by the strategy of creating levels of abstraction.

In Part II, where we illustrate the many forms of joining as relation, there is an example of teaching reading at a three-level structure. The development of such a structure takes as many as 18 to 20 different kinds of works and at least three to four classroom

weeks. In the next part, this kind of development can be found under "Man and Nature." This kind of reading employs the full range of logical processes: joining, separating, judgmental choice (as in an *or* relation), evaluation for class inclusion, multilevel abstraction, extension, and the building of a structure of ideas.

Feeling and cognition

Before embarking on the teaching of joining multiple literary art forms, the teacher is cautioned not to sacrifice the organic, emotional organization of the work of art by which the author would interpret or redeem life. This is often the result when each poem is subjected to an analytic mode which is then turned into the synthetic. But eventually we all must come to it, for synthesis is a need of human existence too; one cannot daily do one's own thing with rock and roll intensity without in time asking what a series of such Woodstocks means, either to oneself or to others who presumably are doing their thing also.

Surely the teacher must ever hold before the pupils any two poems as human creations for other human beings. Each enters into the act of comparison in a more complicated way than do desk and table as human creations, though both poetry and furniture are man-made. For example, a comparison of "The Deacon's Masterpiece" and "The Old Oaken Bucket" (both poems selected here because they refer to the inanimate) might be thought of as joining common emotions rather than two objects. And surely the poems "Four Little Foxes" and "The Pasture" are not to be joined as something only about a baby fox and a colt, for the poems evoke a common tenderness, a sense of the miracle of just being born, rather than being only two poems about animals. On the other hand, if the two poems are joined only as lyrics according to their inner structure, then the joining is about as emotionally neutral as joining desk and table.

In the Oregon curriculum referred to earlier, by the seventh grade the attempt is made to teach the difference between a thing and the meaning of a thing—that which accrues to a thing by human association. The meaning we bring to things or objects or acts or events, rather than the thing or the object or the act or the event, is what reading (the art of literature) is about. The art of joining or synthesizing emotions and meanings within various art forms is a vital aspect of reading as concept development; yet one can sit in a hundred classrooms before one observes a teacher endeavor to join, separate, compare, extend, and synthesize pupils' reactions, values, emotions. It is not correct, thus, to make exposition the sole means of teaching critical thinking; for to compare emotions, to sort out the subtle nuances of feeling, is as logically exacting as determining the degree of necessity in cause and effect. Concept development is not incompatible with the affective domain. Although the teacher may be warned about the sterile effect of teaching cognitive skills for their own sake, all too often the teacher, in the teaching of joining, is tempted to join only the themes of each story or poem or novel or passage instead of joining the meaning of each or joining the pupils' emotional responses to each.

In concept development, the pupil analyzes the text primarily to be able later on to join several works better than if he had not differentiated each one from the others at all. I have observed many, many English classes wherein teachers immediately convert a literary work into thematic analysis; yet the pupils were obviously yearning to discriminate their feelings as well as internalize a concept. And so reading for conceptualization can be an excursion into the development of a wide range of feeling. If English teachers are guilty of subverting feeling while teaching reading, the average reading teacher is usually as remiss, as if dissection—either phonemic or morphological, either in respect to pitch or juncture—is itself the act of reading. Dissection to be sure, but meaning is always more or less elusive. Reading as concept development must always be thought of as creative reading, inasmuch as the pupil in the act of relating has created more than is in each work, more than an assemblage of themes; and the teacher should not consider a pupil's response to be a mere generator for sending logic into orbit. The emotion of the pupil should, of course, generate the conceptualization, but emotion together with its logical refinement has its own existential right to be, or else the act of reading will dry up enjoyment and dampen enlightenment. The pupil should learn the logical processes in reading so that he may better understand emotion and the reason or lack of reason that causes him to cultivate or spurn certain feelings.

The teaching of reading as applied to the literary works discussed in Part Two demonstrates that concept development and the existential counter with literary works are not imcompatible.

Looking backward and forward

Reviewing this demonstration of the theory of concept development raises the question of how it may alter the method of teaching reading.

First, it challenges a traditional list of so-called reading skills as a way to make pupils better readers, especially if thinking is seriously to be considered an integral part of reading; for these fragmentized skills do not sensitize pupils to organic logical processes. Second, it

Teaching reading as concept development

suggests that totally different tests than we now have be devised for measuring the art of reading as synthesis, for present reading tests do not include some of the most important aspects of reading—especially the acts of joining, comparing, developing.

The demonstration deliberately refrained from the use of exposition as subject matter in the teaching of reading because this kind of discourse is not only the favorite but also the conventional one in teaching slow readers to read. In the examples that follow, we show that thinking as a process pervades all forms of discourse. Since we have shown that there need be no incompatibility between a literary confrontation and a logical process, it follows that the widespread separation of the teaching of reading from the teaching of the appreciation of literature is a false dichotomy in method. To us, the experience approach to reading provides the context, while the rhetoric and the logic of reading are used to interpret that context of experience. This view of reading runs through all the examples in the next section.

The additional examples of teaching reading that follow are, therefore, attempts to turn this theory into a teaching method for any classroom grade level. Logical processes are difficult to learn and thus good reading is difficult to learn. For this reason, we believe in a spiral curriculum wherein logical processes are planned to be taught each school year in increasing complexity. To this end in Part 2, a variety of examples has been our aim: 1) in kinds of logical processes, 2) in the number of literary works to be sustained under one concept, 3) in complexity of material, 4) in maturity of the contexual approach, and 5) in length of time devoted to conceptualization.

The experimental and intrepid teacher may want to use these examples as models for the teaching of reading as concept development.

Part two: the practice

Reading readiness: relating things

One way to start teaching for concept building in reading is to provide plenty of practice in comparing concrete objects outside the domain of written language. When the strategy of joining can be readily applied, gradually transfer these skills to literary objects. The writer has worked with youngsters of the middle school in this fashion and discovered that the act of comparing and classification has within it challenging and dramatic exploration, if the objects are within the interest and the maturity of the pupils.

On one occasion in an eighth grade class, I lifted a small, square, four-legged desk, the kind each pupil in the room was using. "What do we call this?" I asked. Every pupil sang out, "A desk." "Why do you call it a desk? What right do you have to call it desk? Prove it is a desk." All sorts of answers came forth: "We sit at them; we write on them; we study at them." The pupils were intuitively resorting to an operational definition worthy of a positivist!

"But in your desks there is no storage beneath the 'object' for your other books. The desks you had last year had a place for your books. Does that feature help make it a desk?" "No." "Yes." All sorts of answers. A few said this about the shelf: "It's not important enough."

"Why not? Who recalls the furniture in Miss Brown's room last year?" It was brought out that in her room the seat and the place for writing were attached as one unit, and underneath was an open shelf for storage. The writing part was slanted too. "Very different, aren't they? Yet you call each a desk."

A pupil added: "And in Miss White's room the *whatever-they-are* are round and four pupils sit at each and write on them and study at them. They are flat and never called *desks*. Always *tables*."

"Well, a study table. Where are we now? When is a desk a *desk*, and a table a *table*? Suppose two of you at lunch time ate at this desk. Would that make it a table? You would have been using it for a table."

I suggested that they recall tables from home: gate-leg tables, drop-leaf tables, dressing tables, corner tables, cocktail tables. Then I asked them to recall roll-top desks and organ desks with their many drawers.

The discussion can be changed from induction at this point to a dictionary search. The teacher should make it clear that the joining has reached an interesting, puzzling phase. Many, many similarities have been discovered, so many that we cannot discover the one or two attributes (Bruner's "exemplars") necessary to tell the difference between a desk and a table. (From the graph, this means, that we have a preponderance of x, but very little, so far, about the a in A and the b in B). If the class is approximately ninth grade level, the teacher might offer the etymological hint that *table* comes from *tavern*. Let the class speculate why. This discussion may lead to the role that use or function plays in definitions, that is, in discovering differences. The important pedagogical focus in all this lesson is, of course, not the correct delineation of *table* from *desk* but the pupil's sensitivity to the strategies of thought involved in joining—the act of relating many similar things is the beginning of developing the concept *desk*.

The spiral curriculum

Elementary school: developing a single genre

The sort of thinking used to prepare for concept building in reading applies as well to composition, very far down in the elementary school. Miss Blanchard, in *The Exchange* (June 1964), provides these examples: "After a discussion about wind in which a first grade class had compared the beneficial, gentle wind with the destructive, harsh wind, one child wrote:

> The gentle wind helps and the harsh wind doesn't. Gentle winds blow the seeds to grow new flowers. The harsh wind blows flowers away.

While another child wrote:

> Sometimes the wind is gentle. It dries clothes and makes the colored clothes look pretty. Sometimes the wind is horrible. It blows snow over the bird food.

Here is another on comparison in which a second grade child combined originality and information in a lesson on comparison:

> Florida shells are as smooth as a baby's skin. Virgin Island shells are bumpity as a stone road. But they are all shells.

A less imaginative child wrote:

> The Virgin Island shells are more colorful than the Florida shells. Most of the Florida shells are white and the other shells are not.

The whole essay by Miss Blanchard should be referred to as a remarkable illustration of a spiral curriculum in the elementary school built around logical processes.

Notice that, as we indicated earlier, in every synthesis of which comparison is one form, there is a going beyond, which means that there is a necessary dependence on imagination and insight. Going beyond is not a distortion or a reliance on incorrect detail; it is a choice of detail, a perception of what details go with or against other details (selecting and excluding). Though some comparisons are better than others, they can seldom be labeled right or wrong. These little compositions based on a kind of joining called comparison are beautiful examples of what we mean. Notice that they are mostly cognitive, except for *gentle* and *horrible*. These examples fall within the experience method of teaching reading; that is, concrete objects within a specific experience, such as a trip, become instigators of thought to which the pupils react orally, and these offerings the teacher transcribes on the board. The pupils then try to read back what they spoke. But the logic of joining goes further, because it tries to have pupils conceptualize the experience, not just report it.

Comparing genres: the concept fable. By third grade, pupils can begin the strategies of joining in such a way that a concept may be more consciously formed. Here is an example of a Delaware teacher who endeavored to develop the concept *fable.* Two fables, "The Hare and the Tortoise" and "The Ant and the Grasshopper," were presented.

In presenting "The Hare and the Tortoise," analytical questions were asked about both animals; then the differences were brought out.

What is the difference between a hare and a rabbit?
What is the difference between a tortoise and a turtle?
Do you suppose that the story could be called "The Rabbit and the Turtle"?

The class was asked to think about the animals as they listened to the story to see if there was any reason why they might like to change the title. An analysis of the behavior of the two animals followed the reading of the story.

Which animal would you like to be if you had a choice? Why?
Which animal seemed to be smarter in the beginning?
What made you think he was smarter?
Did you change your mind about this animal later?
Why did you change your mind?
Can you tell what *wise* means?
Which animal was wise, and how was he wise?
Do you know what *foolish* means?
Is one animal foolish? How?

After using this short, defining, analytical reasoning and some classifying questions, the teacher moved to a hypothetical situation by asking the students to describe themselves as a person behaving like one of the animals—wise or foolish. The teacher invited them to tell a story using two children, one wise and one foolish, who in a situation of the pupils' making behave like the animals in this story.

The next day a new story was written on the board using two animals other than the hare and the tortoise. One animal was slow but wise, while the other was quick but foolish. After the new story had been analyzed well, the teacher initiated a discussion about the meaning of the form of the story. Animals were used to tell a lesson to people. Then the teacher went on inductively with "The Ant and The Grasshopper."

The children all knew what ants and grasshoppers are. Previously, the teacher had read a book about ants, *Insect Engineers,* to them. In the fall, they had collected and examined grasshoppers. Now they were ready to discuss these two insects in terms of behavior. The teacher was ready to ask both hypothetical and opinion questions relating animals to people:

Which insect would you choose to be if you could be one?
Which insect might be happier? Why?
Are people happy for the same reasons?
How do you know?

After reading the story to the class, the teacher asked the pupils to compare this story with the other story, where there were also a wise character and a foolish character.

Do the characters who seem wise in the beginning seem wise at the end of the story?
Was this true of both stories?
Why did you change your mind about one animal and not the other?
What lesson might the two stories be telling us?
How can a story about animals help us to be wiser than we are now?
Going back to "The Hare and the Tortoise," what lesson can we learn from these two animals?
In what ways are the two stories alike?
What makes them both fables? From our paradigm

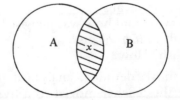

A = story one; B = story two; x = commonality, which becomes, by

Just as sixth grade pupils were asked to distinguish a desk from a table, so our pupils later in the year might compare myth and legend and then relate each to the concept fable. What are the differences? In what way are myths and fables alike? The concept fable is now being further expanded and refined through differentiation. With this new control of form, the pupils could use the fable form creatively to bring out a lesson of their own. If the pupils seem capable at this stage, or perhaps later in the next year, the concept *fable* can be made part of a system:

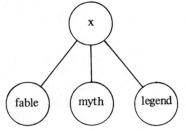

When older, they will be ready for the sophistication of *Gulliver's Travels, Animal Farm,* and *The Saber-Tooth Curriculum.* This is what we mean by a spiral curriculum in reading.

Middle school: relating poems to develop the concept "longing"

Somewhere along the way in the spiral curriculum, the pupil must learn the strategies in joining several things or items or literary works. In attempting this, the teacher should offer help only when pupils stall, and the help should be of the nature of guiding questions. The depth of thought here is not in the questions but in the control of the logical process itself. The reading problem, the teacher can point out, is the same as that of joining and comparing desks and tables. The model may be put on the board as follows:

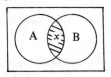

The teacher should ask where and how we begin a search for commonality. Such a search, we found, stirs up considerable excitement and controversy and much pupil interaction. All offerings—however off the mark—should be listed on the board and each should be defended, elaborated, or rejected until the class fuses them into a few alternatives. All during this shifting the pupils should be acquiring the habit of rereading. This phase should not be hurried, for it is a valuable way of learning to read better.

60   *Teaching reading as concept development*

induction, the following: 1) Both are very short; 2) both tell a story; 3) both take place in "never" land; 4) both have animals that speak; 5) both have a "lesson" for people. What are the differences in the two stories that do not go into x? (The x was developed inductively by questioning, not told by the teacher.)

Later, a creative play of each story, developed around the contrast of foolish and wise, was presented. Next they read the "Crane and the Fox," which is an extension of the concept fable.

How does it differ from the other two?
Can it be called a fable anyway? Why?

Finally, each child wrote a fable of his own. With this third story the teacher tested each child without his knowing it, not to give a mark but to perceive to what extent the new tool—the concept *fable*—would be applied to the new situation. In this third case the animals were different, the situation different, the lesson somewhat different, yet the fable form (the x) permitted the joining. Would the pupils sense this similarity? This you may recall is a distance test, in that the test itself is a form of teaching reading and also because it is outside the situation in which it was learned. Within this kind of incipient concept development, Vygotsky (1962) reveals that the teacher should discern how well the two movements of thought in concept development are going on. The teacher may check the process of concept development in this way:

1] An inductive moving toward a generalization while developing the concept fable.

2] A moving out to try the concept on new items, entities, works of art, to see whether they can be absorbed into it or whether the concept itself must be modified. The following diagram may help the teacher in this reaching out, this "going beyond," of the second movement.

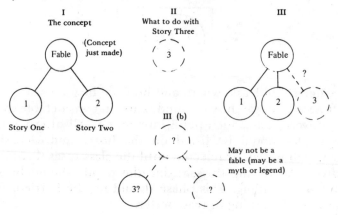

As an illustration, let us take some more poetry and propose a more complex joining in the process of handling as many as three poems. The poem "Romance" expresses a mood that has held every child captive: the yen to get away, to run off; a nostalgia; a longing to break routine. Chimborazo is a mountain and Cotopaxi is a volcano in Ecuador. Popocatapetl is a volcano in Mexico.

ROMANCE

When I was but thirteen or so
    I went into a gold land.
Chimborazo, Cotopaxi
    Took me by the hand.

My father died, my brother too,
    They passed like fleeting dreams,
I stood where Popocatapetl
    In the sunlight gleams.

I dimly heard the master's voice
    And boys far-off at play—
Chimborazo, Cotopaxi
    Had stolen me away.

I walked in a great golden dream
    To and fro from school—
Shining Popocatapetl
    The dusty streets did rule.

I walked home with a gold dark boy
    And never a word I'd say,
Chimborazo, Cotopaxi
    Had taken my speech away.

I gazed entranced upon his face
    Fairer than any flower—
O shining Popocatapetl
    It was thy magic hour.

The houses, people, traffic seemed
    Thin fading dreams by day;
Chimborazo, Cotopaxi,
    They had stolen my soul away!

                — W. J. Turner

Every youngster will relish stanza three, the daydreaming in the master's (teacher's) class, but perhaps few will have been so absorbed as to withdraw from play. (The youngster in this poem "had it bad.") The pupils should be encouraged to swap their runaway dreams, even their actual French leave or playing hooky. The teacher might ask if they had ever felt like the boy or if they thought he finally got to Ecuador or Mexico. Does it matter? Let them run freewheeling through the poem. As the talk subsides, a closer look at

the text may lead the pupils to note the degree of the lad's enthral-
ment, every stanza seeming to contribute more about the strength of
this boy's longing. Can we, from stanza to stanza, trace the progress
or unfolding of this dream? It is like a plot. Logically, each stanza is
an incremental joining. What do the following phrases mean? *Took
me by the hand . . . had stolen me away . . . thy magic hour . . . had
stolen my soul away!* Why the switch from *me* to *soul*? Why is the
word *gold* before *dark boy*? Why are the names *Chimborazo,
Cotopaxi,* and *Popocatapetl* repeated so often? Sing them out in
unison, like *abracadabra.* Does it matter whether we know what they
mean or where they are? Do the sounds of far-away names have a
haunting power? Notice that every stanza has an *I* in it except the
last one. Is this just an accident, or unimportant? In these questions
we are mixing the textual reading with the development of meaning,
not as something linguistic, apart from feeling.

Why does the very last line seem to be a climax, a pulling together of the nature of the dream? Suppose someone came up to you
and said, "I dream a lot about a mountain in South America. It has
stolen my soul away." Why does this statement in isolation seem
drab, but mean more when it caps this poem? It is now more than
just information or description. Why? Let's read the poem aloud
once more. Notice as we go how the rhythm creates a dreamy mood.
What is this mood? How do you know?

Suppose we follow this poem with another, "A Vagabond Song."

A VAGABOND SONG

There is something in the autumn that is native to my blood—
Touch of manner, hint of mood;
And my heart is like a rhyme,
With the yellow and the purple and the crimson keeping time.

The scarlet of the maples can shake me like a cry
Of bugles going by.
And my lonely spirit thrills
To see the frosty asters like a smoke upon the hills.

There is something in October sets the gypsy blood astir;
We must rise and follow her,
When from every hill of flame
She calls and calls each vagabond by name.

— Bliss Carman

This poem, in view of our pedagogy of concept development, was
selected because it is a continuation of the theme of being "called by
nature"—this time in a different way. It is in the differentiation of
the two moods of "Romance" and of "A Vagabond Song" that

greater subtlety in reading is demanded. "Vagabond" must be read for itself as encounter—as an experience to relish, as a feeling to be enjoyed for its own sake in a flash of recognition, and as a fresh tingling flow of emotion. To start, all we need say is to observe your own feelings as you hear the poem unfold. What mood came to you gradually as you read it? What lines seemed to click, to stand out? Why? Was it because in the past, autumn had made some call to you? Any memories? Do all people respond to autumn in this way? Does autumn affect any of you differently from the way this poem does? Only one aspect of autumn seems to appeal here, what is it? Is the speaker justified in comparing *scarlet* to the cry of bugles? *Is* autumn like a parade going by? Why *parade*? What words suggest agitation, excitement? Does autumn drive you generally to a walk in the woods, an auto ride in the country? A stroll through a park? Going camping?

Now let's all reread "Romance." In respect to mood, how can the two be related? How could we say that the Cotopaxi mountains in Ecuador call too? Quietly? Stealthily? How in contrast does autumn call? How can the second mood be described? Can you say that each poem is essentially the same mood? How does each mood enter into the person speaking? What probably is the origin of this boy's romance with Cotopaxi? Would the lad himself know? In "Vagabond" the source is definite—not a long way off. Suppose you lived in the city and had spent your boyhood in wooded country. Would autumn then call forth something closer to "Romance" or to "Vagabond"? Why is the word *vagabond* used? According to the poem's text, is the young boy really a vagabond? Can one feel like a vagabond and not be one? Why is the word *gypsy* used here? How does accessibility or nearness enter into each poem? If Cotopaxi were actually visited or just a mile away, what would happen to the spell? Is one autumn enough? If you have seen one, have you seen them all? How far away from us is autumn when autumn comes? Could both moods reside in the same person? Would longing and nostalgia be different? How could we relate them? Why are the two rhythms different? Could the person in each poem enjoy either Cotopaxi or autumn without ever leaving his home? Would looking at a photograph of Cotopaxi be the same as looking out the window at autumn? Is Cotopaxi native to the blood? If one lived within the sight of Cotopaxi, could it become native to the blood? Why is "Romance" the title? Isn't a vagabond romantic?

One pedagogical purpose of comparing the two poems is to subtly drive the pupil back into the text for closer reading as the relation of the feeling tone in the two poems is explored. In this case, the teacher is trying to bring to the surface the various stances from which comparisons are made. The pupils should now search the poems for overlappings (x) and give the source in them that prompted them to make the similarities. Similarities, pupils should see, in time, are discoveries.

The teacher might now take another poem, "The Lake Isle of Innisfree," to continue the development of the same theme of longing in a slightly different dimension from that in "Romance" and in "A Vagabond Song." Innisfree is a small island in a lake near the poet's Irish home.

THE LAKE ISLE OF INNISFREE

I will arise and go now, and go to Innisfree,
And a small cabin build there, of clay and wattles made;
Nine bean rows will I have there, a hive for the honey bee,
    And live alone in the bee-loud glade.

And I shall have some peace there, for peace comes dropping slow,
Dropping from the veils of the morning to where the cricket sings;
There midnight's all a glimmer, and noon a purple glow,
    And evening full of the linnet's wings.

I will arise and go now, for always night and day
I hear lake water lapping with low sounds by the shore;
While I stand on the roadway, or on the pavements gray,
    I hear it in the deep heart's core.

                   — William Butler Yeats

Before presenting the poem, the teacher could launch it somewhat this way: Recall that in our discussion of "A Vagabond Song" that we posed a situation of this kind: A person who may have been brought up in a wooded land, spending a boyhood climbing hills in autumn, piling up leaves, and watching colored smoke, feels the call of autumn. In this sense, autumn becomes a sort of Cotopaxi. How? But not quite. Why? In respect to Cotopaxi, has the boy been there? Does this third poem also show relation between speaker and place? This will emerge: What it is like to want to go back to a place you already have in your blood. See whether you have ever been haunted in the same way—to yearn to go back where you once were, a kind of reverse homesickness an "awaysickness"—the image of it popping up unexpectedly, again and again, in a busy street, a crowded restaurant, or often at study when things go wrong. Listen to this poem. Does its mood have much in common with many of your moods—with most of us at times? Do we kind of build ourselves into places? Does this poem come close to any feeling of a once-lived-in place you have stirring in you? Were you utterly neutral when you heard this poem? Moods are difficult to talk about, and all three speakers tried to explain the mood they were in; they let you know something about themselves, and in so doing, we learn something about ourselves. Did you ever hear the expression "You can't go home again"? Is it possible that in time the speaker will not be happy, even if he does go back to his island cottage? It is often true that after a few days of peace at camp, instead of enjoying the cricket and the linnet and "lake water lapping," city boys long for the car tires whining and the bustle of strange street crowds. I know a man in his forties who lives in the country but who drives to the city occasionally and walks down an ever-bustling, crowded street, enters an automat, and eats there, watching the people. Why? Because the longing gets strong to return to the sights and sounds of his boyhood days.

Does the speaker indicate why he wants to go back? What does he miss? Can't he have it where he is? An "evening full of the linnet's wings," what possibly could the speaker mean? How can we hear something "in the deep heart's core"? Guess what the word *glade* means. Is the mood here closer to that of "A Vagabond Song" or "Romance"? Notice, now, the three different places that call forth or evoke different reactions or moods. What is peculiar about the description of Chimborazo and Cotopaxi in relation to that of autumn or Innisfree? Go back to the poem and note how each place is handled. The pupils should now discover how little the mountains are described at all. How literally are they described? Why doesn't the speaker go into some detail to show what there was that attracted him so very much? The other two speakers did just that, a good many details given about autumn and about the boyhood dwelling as justification or reason for leaving where they are. Why is this? Which poem is most definite and concrete in detail? Why? Does this give us a clue to the kind of mood the poem "Romance" sets up in relation to the other two? Could all three poems be called romantic, each in a different way? Are the three moods the same? Judging from these poems only, what does romantic mean?

Let's now turn to our model for help. How would you go about filling it in?

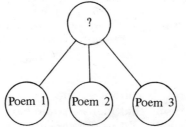

Suppose we altered the question mark to *mood*, to *structure*, to *calling*, to *places*, or to *my reaction*. How would each of these purposes alter our looking at the three poems as a whole? Try joining the three poems in some way of your own. Some teachers may want to do this with the entire class; some may want to turn it over to committees. Notice that the pupils now must reread each poem, but in a different way.

Now that we have discovered and invented several ways of joining the three poems by means of comparison, let's see what meeting another poem, "The Shell," would do to our evolving structure.

THE SHELL

And then I pressed the shell
Close to my ear
And listened well,
And straightway like a bell
Came low and clear
The slow, sad murmur of the distant seas,
Whipped by an icy breeze
Upon a shore
Wind-swept and desolate.
It was a sunless strand that never bore
The footprint of a man,
Nor felt the weight
Since time began
Of any human quality or stir
Save what the dreary winds and waves incur.
And in the hush of waters was the sound
Of pebbles rolling round,
Forever rolling with a hollow sound.
And bubbling sea-weeds as the waters go,
Swish to and fro
Their long, cold tentacles of slimy grey.
There was no day,
Nor ever came a night
Setting the stars alight
To wonder at the moon:
Was twilight only and the frightened croon,
Smitten to whimpers, of the dreary wind
And waves that journeyed blind—
And then I loosed my ear. . . .O, it was sweet
To hear a cart go jolting down the street.

— James Stephens

Is this other poem also about getting away from it all? Let's look at it, first, as a poem, one that many people have enjoyed. You know the legend that a seashell held to the ear calls up the sound of the sea and the beach where it was found. Can you single out the mood? Is there a call? Does the speaker accept the call? Is it possible for a

Teaching reading as concept development

peculiar sound—like *jolting*—to stand for a kind of continuing experience we hold dear? For instance, a slammed car door at night announces the arrival of expected friends, the flapping wings of geese overhead, the arrival of fall. Did the speaker really hear in the shell all that he set forth? Would another listener have heard and felt other sensations? Would you? Might the cart be a sound of boredom to others? Is there any clue why he did not accept the romance that the shell offers? Some people do not like to move out of their circle of existence, finding pleasure in limited but safe surroundings. I once met a man who said that on one July Fourth he sat in a hot bath and read the morning newspaper, and it was much more fun than going out to the Grand Canyon. Is the speaker in the poem adventurous? Does the dramatic contrast at the end pull us inside the speaker's view so that we are suspended for a moment within his experience, though we may not ourselves react in his way? Did you feel caught up in the desolation? Why?

Let's look at this poem now in relation to the other three poems. How should we proceed? How could it be fitted in? If the class has initial trouble in responding, the teacher might suggest these aids: Has there been any hint of rejection in the other three poems? Is there almost a complete surrender in the other three? Do all four have response to a call? Do all have longing? How does "Romance" differ from the other three and yet partake of something in "The Shell"? How does "The Shell" differ from all the others? Of all four poems, which is the most difficult to be joined with the others? In all four do the speakers reach the place that they are longing for or that really is the source of the mood? In these poems is there active participation in the place, except through memory, dreams, or imagination? Are the speakers actually participating? Which one comes closest to it? To what extent are our lives lived in dreaming about what we hope to do or in reliving what we have done? Should we enjoy our memories, wishes, anticipations, recollections as much as our actual doing? Is there a danger in living solely in either way? (Some years later, in the upper school years, this concept will be developed as a philosophy, in Wordsworth.)

Testing by extension. The teacher should endeavor at times to determine how well these strategies of joining are being absorbed. This kind of testing should be a learning device to strengthen the logical process, not one by which to grade the pupils. To do this at this stage of the development of the concept of "longing for some place beyond the present," a fifth poem such as "Sea Fever" may be read together in class.

SEA FEVER

I must down to the seas again, to the lonely sea and the sky,
And all I ask is a tall ship and a star to steer her by,
And the wheel's kick and the wind's song and the white sail's
    shaking,
And a grey mist on the sea's face and a grey dawn breaking.

I must down to the seas again, for the call of the running tide
Is a wild call and a clear call that may not be denied;
And all I ask is a windy day with the white clouds flying,
And the flung spray and the blown spume, and the sea-gulls crying.

I must down to the seas again to the vagrant gypsy life.
To the gull's way and the whale's way where the wind's like a
    whetted knife;
And all I ask is a merry yarn from a laughing fellow-rover,
And quiet sleep and a sweet dream when the long trick's over.

                                       — John Masefield

Either after analysis in the manner of the previous poems or, depending on how independent the pupils are taught to be, without class analysis at all the teacher may say, "How, without any help from me, would you try to fit this new poem into our growing structure? Let's recall our structure so far.

Our problem will   Why are the dotted
look like this: lines leading out to 5?

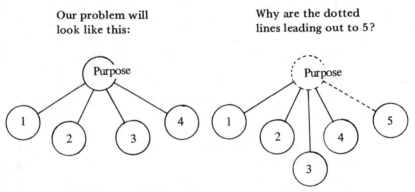

The following should emerge from discussion and not be *told* to the pupils. First, we do not yet know the nature of number five. Second, we do not know whether it belongs with the other four. Third, if it can be made to fit some, as yet not-thought-out, purpose we should still try to reveal its special difference from the other four. Fourth, we may have to reject it as an impossible fit. Remember our task model some time ago? Can it help you with the problem? The teacher may review the model on the board with the help of the pupils. See whether you could write a paragraph on how you would deal with "Sea Fever" in relation to the other four poems. Afterward we will exchange our ideas as we have worked them out in writing.

Do not put an individual grade on each paper. Give the individuals in the class the feeling of examining as a class their own success with joining. Look closely at the logical strategies in the compositions. What individual troubles in joining were experienced? Where were the weaknesses? How good were the various attempts at synthesis? After the class has shared its offerings informally and perhaps even come to some conclusions as to the possible modes of joining—some students naturally passing through several fluctuating changes in interpretation—the teacher may then enter in to guide the interplay of thought. Is "Sea Fever," like all the other poems, setting up a place longed for, a place not reached? Was the speaker ever there, as was the speaker in "Innisfree"? Of the five poems, which one really is the hardest to fit and in one respect may be taken out of the structure?

Somebody may want to play around with the inner form and rhythm of each; for each poem has something quite dramatic of its own, and each has its appropriate rhythm. Which forms are more alike? Which are quite different? Do all these poems deal with a discontent with present living? Are all the speakers under some kind of spell? Which one seems to comment on his own life? Could somebody in class have experienced all five of these moods? From reading these five poems what could we reasonably conclude about human beings? Some brighter youngster may like to join the five poems into this kind of structure:

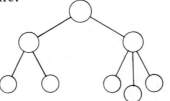

If this kind of diagram appears formidable and alien to literary thinking, we can suggest this more familiar scheme to fill in:

I.
   A.
      1.
      2.
   B.
      1.
      2.
      3.

High school: differentiating three poems on the same subject

Differentiation within sameness. Christopher Boyle, of St. Andrews School in Delaware, teaches a deliberately unstructured unit called American and British Poetry. I say *unstructured* because there is by plan no overall theme, no chronological order, no necessary relation to periods, no following of trends; there is a variety of subjects and a variety of authors—all leading, hopefully, toward enjoyment and appreciation. But within this general study of poetry, he has arranged several groups of poems, to be taught together in his own pedagogical design. One group is composed of three mouse poems: "To a Mouse," by Burns; "Meadow Mouse," by Roethke; "Ballad of a Mouse," by Wallace. Let me quote from Boyle's letter to me:

> I guess what I am after is what you would call concept formation, even, perhaps, a historical generalization. In the first poem, I try to get the students to see the clear "social union" between the man and the mouse, the fact that the man can address the mouse as a fellow creature, and thus they have a dramatic relationship to each other. What separates them is, of course, that the man has hindsight and foresight; and this keeps man out of a perfect social union with nature's creatures, though he seems to want to belong. In the second poem, the confrontation here is of a would-be savior to his victim; there is again a sort of relationship between man and mouse, though one of unequals. What separates them here, though, is a kind of natural mystery: that the mouse, despite the dangers in the world, would prefer the world to the man's protection. Why is this, the man seems to ask, and then goes on to make the world's dangers for the mouse lead into thoughts about other helpless creatures, including man. Thus, the man in this poem is partly in nature's social union in being like the mouse in his helplessness, but out of the union in his being unable to force the mouse to accept his loving protection. So far, as you can see, the poem is unlocked by the clear speaker-audience relationship between man and mouse; in both poems the man speaks *of* and *to* a mouse he has confronted and is both *of* the nature which includes the mouse and *out of* this nature. The third poem, I always start with a suggestion that the students try to determine whether the speaker in the poem is the same man as the shooter of the mouse. They have a hard time with this, since the poem has a peculiar vagueness about the speaker: at some times he seems to be in the mouse's head, and there is not anywhere in the poem an "I" who can be without doubt called the actor in the poem. At any rate, this poem shows no union between mouse and man at all. The man is alone at the end, foolish and furious, at himself presumably; the mouse is also alone in his suffering. Everything here is chaos, disorder and separateness—a grotesque incident only. The diction of the poem establishes it as modern, and one might hazard some sort of idea here about modern man's aloofness from nature and irrational barbarity to the mouse, though this probably shouldn't be pushed too far. Clearly, though, the relationship between man and mouse is nothing like that of the other two poems; there is an even greater mystery about what separates man from mouse here than there was in the other two poems. One might even see some sort of sequence here in terms of historical alienation from nature that seems peculiarly ours these days.

I quote in length to note that Boyle is conceptualizing the three poems into something like an interpretation, which is to say, logically, a relation of relations. He told me, "I want them to see that a man's character can be revealed by the way he looks at an animal, and this in turn provides a clue to man's relation to nature." Such a teacher is not content always to teach a number of poems discretely; rather he groups them so as not to encourage a light, touch-and-go flitting from likeness to likeness, from difference to difference; and then he has the students seek the character of the group of poems as a group. He leads the pupil's ideas up a ladder of abstraction. He knows where he is going logically as well as rhetorically and syntactically, for he concludes,

> I've left out here all the obvious particular features of each poem, especially the peculiar quatrains of the third poem and its harsh rhythms, both of which seem to me to contribute to the overall effect. These should be brought up as the students look at each poem, for implicit in this whole procedure is that each poem is studied *first* by itself, though naturally students can't help bringing insights from one poem to another poem.

College: relating three poems on a flower
in differing historical periods

Another kind of design for teaching reading as concept development is described by Craig (1965) who taught it in his college classes at Amherst. He established a context called "Theme and History: Three Poets on a Single Theme"—Henry King's "Contemplation Upon Flowers," the seventeenth century; Christopher Smart's "On a Bed of Guernsey Lillies," the eighteenth century; Wordsworth's "The Small Celandine," the early nineteenth century. This undertaking in reading is not an analysis of each in respect to its rhetorical or aesthetic form but in respect to the relation of each speaker to the flower. "Each poem presents a situation in which the speaker considers himself as he meditates upon some flowers." He writes:

> Now it is clear enough at first glance that each of these poems is in a general way about man and nature certainly one of the largest subjects in English poetry from the days when April was the time when longen folk to goon on pilgrymages to those when it has become the cruellest month. (p. 288)

And much later he comments on the reader's

> . . . inescapable knowledge that whatever their similarities may be these are three poems in three quite different idioms, and that they could no more be the same, or "say the same thing," than any of us can really live and think and breathe in seventeenth-, eighteenth-, or early nineteenth-century England. (p. 293)

He finally brings the logic of preference (comparison) back to the affective realm:

> In other words, even if we do persist, even if we do declare ourselves as ranking one of these poems over the other two, we cannot fail to discover something about ourselves, about the values and assumptions that matter most to us. (p. 294)

He also suggests other thematic juxtapositions to elicit the full reading of each one in relation to the others:

> I recall the delight with which a colleague of mine once juxtaposed Dylan Thomas' "The Force That Through the Green Fuse Drives the Flower" with a passage from Thomson's "Spring" and a poem by Henry Vaughan entitled "The Evening Watch": it taught him, he said, among other things, what the Thomas poem was really about. I recently found it highly instructive to myself and to my students to set for them an essay on Robert Browning's "Prospice," Hardy's "The Darkling Thrush," and Yeats' "An Acre of Grass." In each of these poems, as you may recall, the speaker is at the end of life, or at the end of a phase of life that has exhausted him. (p. 294)

Relating two relationships

Two short stories on father-son relationship

So far, the subject matter for our teaching of concept development through reading has been purposely confined to poetry, simply because the lyric, being short and subjective (being close to the autistic character of the young), is more easily handled within the limit of daily lessons. The relating of short stories and, *a fortiori,* plays and novels, takes more time; for the story is not only longer but demands more sustained attention. Just as the poem is taught primarily for engagement so the story must be allowed to work its mysterious impact on various, differing pupils. Trading their various responses should be integral to the reading.

The analytical stage in comparing stories is often obstructed by the very fact that it is difficult to hold a story of from six to ten pages in the head as an organic entity, and then, while doing so, to compare this entity to one from another story equally long. Although it tends to be the stock in trade of literary appreciation in most classrooms, to allow pupils to compare only in general two themes abstracted from the two stories is not to teach the total act of reading. It is only to tolerate, as Blanchard states it, "a roving eye for resemblances." Reading for concept development forces the pupil back to the two texts, because then reading becomes an act of progressively synthesizing thought serially in time. To illustrate, these two stories are selected: "The Erne from the Coast" (Beachcroft) and "A Really Important Person" (Chute), both found in Certner and Henry, *Short Stories for Our Times* (1950). The two stories are presented here in skeletal form to help the reader understand the inherent task of comparing them.*

*These two stories are taken from a larger concept to be developed called *Within the Family*. Henry and Certner, the editors, include two other stories in order to clarify and delineate the concept—Morley Callaghau's "All the Years of Her Life," and Francis M. Frost's "The Heart Being Perished."

A robust farmer, proud of his vigor, continually taunts his frail son whose passivity does not seem to measure up to his thirteen years. On one occasion, while guarding the sheep, the son could not prevent an eagle from flying off with a new-born lamb. The furious father would not believe the boy's story and charges him with cowardice and negligence. At the next watch, the sheep are again assaulted by the eagle, now grown doubly bold, but this time the boy deliberately engaged the hugh erne in bloody battle: his face clawed, his chest torn open, the boy hoisted the dead bird over his shoulders and dragged his way to the farm house. The jubilant father honors his son at the pub and, back home, even escorts him to the bedroom door. (T. O. Beachcroft, *The Erne from the Coast.*)

A policeman is worried by his son's unresponsiveness at home and his reluctance to talk, even about school. Later, unknown to the boy, the mother by chance comes upon a school composition on the assignment "The Most Important Person I Know." The boy had selected his own father! On the job the father is like a different person, cheerful to all his fellow workers, glad to live up to his son's appraisal of him. (B. J. Chute, *A Really Important Person.*)

The response to the first story will leave some kind of assimilated deposit in the consciousness of each pupil, and the class might try to make explicit what it is, allowing for dissenters and always returning to the text to clarify their inchoate ideas. The second story is to be read for its own sake, in the same way; that is, for the quality of its encounter. It too leaves some stirring, some memory trace, in consciousness. Again we ask the pupils to put into words what it seems to be.

Next, the teacher invites a relating of the two verbally phrased traces or responses, written and/or oral. As a preliminary, the teacher accepts a rough-hewn, roving eye overlap, such as the notation that both stories deal with the tension or conflict or the gap between a father and a son. In each story, for some implicit reason, all is just not quite right between them. The teacher may ask what the origin of the tension in each story is as well as what is its nature. Few pupils, if any, can answer these except fuzzily; the teacher then must resort to the text of each story, being compelled to have the pupils not only reread but to read differently. For instance, in the first story the pupils are led to discover that it is the boy's story—his trying to repair or change his father's attitude. In the second, it is the father's story—his worry over his not being close to his son. In both, there is a reconciliation; and in both, the son's actions reduce the tension. These are the overlap x in our thought model. In order to discriminate the stories, A and B in our model, the teacher then asks what light these two tensions—that between policeman and son and that between farmer and son—and especially the events of the reconciliation, shed on father-son relations that are not directly in either story. In other words, how can they be grafted or joined in such a manner that the interpretation is bigger than either story?

The pupils might write out such interpretations, or the teacher might put the pupils' interpretations on the board to help them create the synthesis, nudging them by appropriate questioning to turn again and again to the two texts for support. A good synthesis always has identifiable elements from both things (stories) brought together, but the combination always contains something important that is not wholly in either. Abstraction thus sets in at this stage because synthesis is possible only by leaping beyond the facts: checking the fact level at this stage will not change the quality of the synthesis. At this stage, the return to the text is a *test of the synthesis*; a fact taken from the texts is reviewed carefully to determine its correctness, not in terms of its truth but in terms of its presence there in the story or of its use by a pupil. Notice that the questions framed by the teacher at this stage are not the usual prepared questions called *study guides*; nor are they the levels of cognition taxonomy, like Bloom's (1956), designed to insure that we have a range of high, middle, and low thought questions to make pupils think. There is a dynamic, controlling mode of inquiry. Since our context is already beyond the comparison dimension of joining, in order to effect a synthesis, the questioning cannot drop down to the finicky, factual, recall level; fact questions, if necessary now, only help teachers push along the hypothetical, problematic quest as a thinking goal.

In *Erne* the apprehension runs from the son to the father, for Harry feels he must earn his father's admiration. From the evidence in the story, however, the father does not seem to be anxious about his son's view of him. In the second story the father, too, is concerned about his son's shortcomings; but in contrast to Harry's father, he wants to help him personally and seeks to do so, for he is a bit worried about where he stands in his son's affection. The problem of synthesis is to help the student ascertain what the two stories together offer that each read separately does not. This quest demands a rereading—a very specific, purposeful reading. Here, at this point, the creative powers of the student are brought into play by launching some trial joinings. One student in the tenth grade worked out a joining of the two that looked like this:

> In the course of living together as a family uneasyness arises sometimes between a father and a son. In these two stories neither fathers seem to be liking the way their sons are shaping up. Fathers have an ideal of what a son should be like and try to mould the boy that way. But sons dream for a life of their own and are in conflict with their fathers about

this. Sometimes this is brought out in what is half-said. A feeling is present but it is not talked out. This is true of both stories. In *Erne* it is the son that silently tries to help the situation. In the second, it is the father. In each story because of some act by each son the father and son are brought closer than ever before. In the second story the boy did not know anything was wrong with himself and in the first the son and the father knew. In the first story I wish the father had put his arms around him or hugged him or something.

After a pupil's synthesis has been read aloud to the class, the teacher may press further with hypothetical questions of this kind: Suppose the father had never got to read this homework? Wasn't the boy's love for him still there? Suppose Harry had not killed the huge bird, but it had escaped, and suppose Harry had returned wounded just as he was, without the proof. Why didn't Harry's father seek to discover qualities in his son besides physical courage?

The teacher may notice that, at this stage of reading, the type of questions employed in joining or in relating are more interpretive and hypothetical. This kind of questioning is permissible only when through discussion there is a concrete base of fact and the inner relations of each story are already established through analysis. At this level of abstraction, the emotional impact of each story as initially experienced slowly weakens, as with us all. But even at this level of conceptual development, it can be partially revived by a certain kind of questioning that joins and compares, using certain emotional passages in each story as illustrations.

There is the rereading of that delicious mood when Harry's father showed him personally to the bedroom door with a special tone in his goodnight. How deep Harry must have slept that night and what a wonderfully new morning to arise to! Then, in comparison, to reread the last line of the second story, the father's joyous feeling—how good to have a good son! For this very reason, he is sharing in the joy of the coming baby of his fellow policeman. These are great moments in life, these sudden dawnings of love. Here, two faces of love are being compared. And here, too, fuse the cognitive and affective sides of our being. In this way, the teacher may protect the work from both too much dissection and conceptualization, and on the other hand, too much freewheeling in general ideas. He thus keeps before the pupil the fullness of reading. Actually, then, dissection (analysis) and conceptualization (synthesis) need not murder the story or rarify the feeling potential if the teacher handles the act of comparing as we suggest here.

Reading as relation

Relating full length works

Since the 1940s, Nobel and Noble have been publishing *Comparative Classics,* a series of texts, each volume of which presents an older classic with a modern one of the same type for a comparative study. Usually, the two works are alike in literary form and in situation, sometimes, roughly, in theme. Perhaps we owe to this innovation the conceptually planned curriculum that often brings together *Romeo and Juliet* and *West Side Story* or *An Enemy of the People* and *The Crucible.* But even with this as a basis, when conventionally trained teachers bring together two literary works in this way, the comparison is usually loose, swinging back and forth from paired likenesses to paired contrasts, rarely moving toward a synthesis by a conceptualization of the two in terms of the strategies of the new logic. For instance, in the 1960 volume of *Comparative Classics,* which uses *A Tale of Two Cities* and *The Moon is Down,* the act of comparison comprises two pages of 23 questions, and of course no concept that serves to join the two novels can emerge from such a miscellany. No structure of relations could possibly evolve from the 23 questions; a pupil's answering correctly 23 questions in a row does not lead to a conceptual structure to be tested by closer reading.

Despite this weakness, the treatment is a step in the right direction. I have made use of the publisher's volume on *Macbeth* and *The Emperor Jones* in terms of the Whiteheadian logic of relations. Several student teachers under my direction have tried out the new logic described here with these comparisons, *The Great Gatsby* and *Raisin in the Sun* as facets of the American Dream. Others have proposed this task: In what way can *Antigone* and *A Man For All Seasons* be linked? Is it worthwhile to try joining them? On what grounds?

At the junior high level, a Florida State experiment (1969) brought together the myth of Prometheus and the novels *Shane* and

Swiftwater—all three tied together by a hero who feels called upon to accept a sacrificial burden for his people. This conceptualization moves through two questions: How is such a man in each a hero? What do they have in common? The worth of this kind of pedagogical undertaking depends on the teacher's sophistication in the strategy of synthesis, the operations he teaches in the act of comparison, and the realization that a concept is an outcome—a structure of relations.

Developing the concept of personal identity. This kind of handling of concept development can be found also in Feidelson (1965), who at Yale has worked with the concept of personal identity in American literature. He says:

> Undoubtedly, the naive, spontaneous way to read a book is to read it solely for itself. But I suppose that the task of the teacher is somehow to push students beyond their pristine innocence—many kinds of innocence, as we know, but in this case the innocence of reading without a context. A teacher, without destroying that naive joy, must divert it into the study of relations, comparisons, and contrasts. Only when we begin to relate, to pair and then to group writers, either explicitly or by implication, does the study of literature properly begin. (p. 276)

He then particularizes in this way, "I suspect that beneath the diverse subjects of American books, there is always this common preoccupation with 'Americanness'; and in this sense American literature positively demands in large-scale study, comparison and contrast of writers, rather than emphasis upon separate authors or works." (p. 277) He next comes down to a piece of "Americanness." It is simply this: *"What is a person?"* Within an established context which he calls "Three Views of the Human Person," he would have the students read *The Scarlet Letter, Walden,* and *The Red Badge of Courage.* He then leads the students through the psychic labyrinth of three persons—Hester Prynne, Henry Thoreau, and Henry Fleming—and finally projects a synthesis. The extended inquiry is not to find out the relative merits of what the three achieved in the worldly sense but to learn that in "their common predicament and their honest dealing with it . . . it is our predicament as well. They had to find out what it meant to be an American. . . ." (p. 284) This return to the self of the reader, after a long logical analysis and then a synthesis, reveals that the cognitive domain can eventually be folded into the affective domain, that the two are not irreconcilable. For the self of the American in these turbulent times is going through an excruciating search for identity and meaning similar to that of these three heroes of other times. The student as symbolic hero is comparing himself with, putting himself against, three other persons of three other times.

Conceptualizing three biographies. Another approach to a continuing topic was used by Curwin (1965) at Philips Exeter. He set up
the context—how do we interpret a life? He then sketched in the
nature of the elements in the context, giving the pupils considerable
leeway but some guidance to erect a structure of their own within
this established frame. He used Boswell's *Life of Johnson,* a life in
which the writer participated almost entirely at first hand; Elizabeth
Bowen's *Yankee from Olympus,* a life that had to be resurrected by
research; and Moss Hart's *Act One,* a life drawn from one's own self.
This established context frees the students to set up strategies to
determine what in our model is *x* and what the essential differences
are in *A, B,* and *C.* What are the pitfalls in gathering data for each
kind of writing and what is the strength of each? Not only are there
three different careers here, but three different historical periods.
How can we evaluate the life lived and at the same time evaluate the
worth of the work as art? Very bright selected seniors are called
upon to handle such difficult questions. Of course, within the given
logical inquiry, many insights into human nature may existentially
strike an individual pupil along the way—insights sometimes more
powerful than the rationally created structure itself.

Conceptualizing within three literary forms. Edward H. Rosen-
berry, of the University of Delaware, once gave a course called "The
Literature of the Sea." He writes, "At least it gets literary study out
of some of its traditional boxes," and it threw a good deal of the
needed conceptualization of this wide-ranging subject onto the students, who not only selected a project that essays to frame a context
to hold some of the works together, but also answered the questions,
"What theme or approach do the *Old Man and the Sea, Man of Aran,*
and *Riders to the Sea* have in common? In what important ways do
they differ?" I should predict that any student coming out of elementary and secondary school with practice in reading as concept
development would immediately use the proper strategies implicit in
such a logical task. And, hopefully, English majors, as future
teachers, taking such a course taught in this way will have been made
aware of a method of teaching that may encourage conceptual reading in their own high school charges.

I learned that this is not now the case from my experience of a
decade in grading the essays submitted as answers to questions of
both the College Entrance Examinations and the Merit Award Con-
tests of the National Council of Teachers of English. These highly
selected writers usually had very good sentence structure and had
read the works intelligently, but they failed conspicuously in
handling the logical strategies of comparison and particularly the
logic of uniting several works under a concept of their own chosing.

All the examples referred to so far represent the kind of teaching of concept development that one may think of as the simultaneous play of spontaneity and structure. Of course, to assign three plays or three novels to be read before they are to be interpreted at all in class is formidable even for bright youth, because this kind of reading will be largely aimless and wasteful unless the teacher has suggested or has worked out with the students the problematic nature of the task. To set down syllabus-like directions, however, violates concept development if it defers the exchange of thought in the classroom for several weeks and, more importantly, lacks a conceptual task. The best plan is to have the students state the problem, and then to present the works serially, to develop gradually the dimensions of the task.

Often in the module scheduling of English, the teacher puts before the pupils a highly structured, rational outline amounting almost to a programed set of questions—all of which is labeled independent study. But this is not independent study; it is individual study. Such an algorithmic method is not concept development. The irony here is that within an innovative, radical schedule of classes there is an ultra-conservative, homemade, mimeographed text with stated directives, all smacking of an 1890 treatment of classics. Reading as concept development is, of course, stifled by tight, prearranged programing of this sort.

In contrast, a good classroom is a flow of ongoing logical processes from day to day within some context that the pupils have invented and are aware of. A previously well-defined context charts a differentiating course for the reading to take, but the logical process itself will remain the same.

Levels of difficulty in concept development. In this kind of teacher-pupil planning, complexity or difficulty is the degree of immersion in a situation. *Difficulty* here does not mean the density or the demands of the reading material (say, "Tintern Abbey" or "We are Seven") but the strain or burden of handling the oncoming material within a needed logical process. One can identify three phases of difficulty by the way the content or subject matter (the reading) is encountered. This would apply to anybody—pupil, researcher, critic.

1. The material (literary works) may be encountered serially, one work at a time, but grouped beforehand, as ours is done in the development of Man and Nature. The pupil has to discover the groupings and join the groupings inherent in the twelve works.

2. A more difficult task is to encounter 10 to 12 previously unread works simultaneously (before discussion), from which an order or structure is to be extracted according to some context de-

cided upon by the recipient (the pupil) as he selects themes, on his own, one by one. It would be interesting to observe some teacher teaching reading in this way. I have never known any teacher to do so, yet we all must meet this kind of piled on, unsorted reading as we go through life.

3. Still more difficult is the encounter with a series of 10 to 12 works presented to the pupil one by one in a miscellaneous or random fashion, from which the pupil is to invent an order, without any clue. This task is somewhat in the manner of Bruner's experiment in *The Process of Thinking.* If some clue to order is not arrived at by the end of the series, it tends to revert to the second kind of encounter, and then later on to the first kind, for it is now a layout of the pupils' own making.

If the pupil looks up a clue to the structure in some reference or critical review, it becomes still easier. And if the structure is created by the teacher and its principle of order presented in full view in a hand-out, and then if the teacher leads the pupil by means of daily lectures through this preplanned order, the logical strain is still less. A pupil should have experience with all these levels of difficulty as he passes through the reading of literature in our schools. How to deal conceptually with serially presented, unordered reading material can be undertaken in the elementary school, and spiraled upward into middle school and beyond.

Conceptualization and writing

This kind of reading promotes better writing too. In a beautiful essay, Evans (1959) sorts out the difference between writing and composing; he shows how a pupil may have a good beginning and ending, a body with unity and coherence, paragraphs with a topic sentence, and sentences well shaped and varied—and yet have nothing to say. The thought is not developed because the concepts are loosely structured. The teacher should be aware that conceptual development is not the same thing as the development of a composition for presentation: on the other hand, a workout in concept development always improves the organization of a paragraph. In large part, good syntax and rhetoric are outcomes of conceptualization, not the other way round.

The formal study of unity and coherence in writing seldom improves composing as much as the progressive development of the concept to be written about. From my own experience with high school seniors, I found that students not formally taught the topic sentence wrote better unified paragraphs after the kind of reading suggested in the above examples of concept development.

Some pedagogical warnings

In English classes we often find two extremes of reading instruction: 1) a kind of wide and varied spontaneous reading of whatever strikes the pupil or whatever the teacher elects to teach, 2) an overstructured guide sheet or syllabus which the pupil must follow according to the way the thought is ordered and the readings assigned. Neither of these can be defined as concept development. If either is to be pedagogically justified, each must be on other grounds.

When the kind of design for teaching reading proposed here is used in the high school, any one of the following three weaknesses may inadvertently creep in: 1) the concepts to be developed may be beyond the present perceptual acuteness of the pupils, so that they cannot experience the logical relations; 2) the process is so loosely and fitfully pursued that the discipline of it does not lead to better control of the operators and strategies in doing future tasks of synthesis; 3) and, above all, the inherent abstract level of the task is too great for any coping with the required generalization. Recently, I taped a teacher who had the pupils read *Crime and Punishment, An American Tragedy,* and Camus' *The Stranger* within the context of three murderers in three novels. There were tangential comparisons of motives, but no reference to the culture in which each murder was done; there was only a discussion of murder in general, as if murder is murder. No effort was made to show that each author used the murder for exploring what values are implied when one person destroys another, whether from a view of self, the nature of society, or one's religious outlook. There was no fundamental reason advanced for probing these three characters.

Another teacher whom I taped simply attempted too much synthesis under impossible conditions of time and process. One committee of five pupils, like three other committees in the class, was to fuse five novels in some way, with each pupil on a committee responsible for one novel but no one pupil having read them all. Pupils were thus making comparisons of novels which they learned about not by reading but by hearing them discussed by the pupil who had. The task was simply overwhelming. This method may be justified perhaps on some other grounds, but not on reading as concept development.

It is fairly common to observe teachers who permit the following kind of pedagogical situation in respect to reading: each of 20 pupils in a class reads a novel and reports to the class on the common assignment, How did the main character change and what was the reason for the change? This is an excellent assignment in order to set up purposive reading, but to ask a class in two discussion periods to pull out a generalization about character change based on 10 oral class reports of 10 minutes or so (each pupil not having read 19 of the books) is to invite vapid abstractions even though the inductive method is used. The exercise might be good for each student to do if used as an opportunity to read independently several books for practice in generalization; but conceived as a lesson, it is not much of an exercise in reading for concept development. This observation is not to condemn the presentation of a series of book reports around a common purpose, but it is intended to criticize the identification of this method with reading for concept development. We want the pupil to be a better reader in that he himself must conceptualize the material by the use of available strategies; but a series of book reports, even on the same theme, is not practice in conceptualization.

Reading as structuring

Joining multiple genres over a longer period of time

At this point, a review of all these applications of concept development presented so far may make it clear how this kind of teaching of reading differs from the traditional or conventional skills approach to reading. The following notations may delineate the two and therefore become a guide to teaching a much larger unit by means of concept development.

1. Not only does the pupil hunt for main and subordinate ideas; he looks for internal relations in each work in order to relate them to another work.

2. Not only does the pupil search for a theme; he notes as well the situation that contains the theme, and he proposes a larger context for that situation.

3. Not only does he read the work as an organic whole; he reads it in light of the works that he read before.

4. Not only does he think incidentally while extracting content; he thinks upon his mode of thinking and how he is reading.

5. Not only does he acquire knowledge; he learns to perform the strategies of thinking; the way ideas have to be joined, separated, discarded, implied, and abstracted in forming a concept. These become part of the meaning of the concept. Bridgman (1959) says about this: ". . . the object of knowledge is not to be separated . . . from the method by which knowledge is acquired." (p. 169)

Inventing a structure of several levels of abstraction

How would the above five characteristics of concept development be used when the number of works may run to 12 or more, may vary in genre and mode, and may consume four to six weeks of classroom time?

As noted in the *English Journal* (Henry, December 1968), the kind of preplanning needed for this kind of teaching of reading is not guided so much by content (as supremely important as it is) as by the nature of the logical process we wish the pupils to experience. In respect to method, the following points would guide the teaching:

1] The structure would not be revealed to the students, not gone over point by point; for the structure is to be invented by them to form the content that is being presented serially day by day.

2] The material to be taught would be deliberately put before the students in such a way that thought processes become integral to the learning of the ideas, thus avoiding the sprawling nature of the progressive unit.

3] The teacher would try to make sure that the concept would be taught in a tentative, hypothetical atmosphere, knowing full well that three weeks will allow but a partial and limited view of "man and nature," and that measurement of the students' understanding of the relation would have to be devised within and be compatible with this atmosphere. Our aim, in sum, is to bring about an assimilation of the relation of the ideas, not a retention of something called "content."

From our experience since 1968, we propose still another:

4] The students would be taught how to deal with levels of abstraction.

Let us try to convert the above method into its needed logical processes:

1] There will be combining and separating—that is, joining apparent opposites while discriminating among close likenesses; from this interplay there will emerge a tentative classification, a set of relations.

2] This class will be expanded by testing it with new cases.

3] Other classes will be created by comparing and excluding; then evaluating new instances—whether they belong to the former class or to a trial new class.

4] There will be an attempt to relate these newly formed classes by a higher abstraction than those that now hold the classes together.

5] The product is a lattice or structure of relations: this is the concept as developed on the basis of the instances and classes dealt with.

6] This concept is now an instrument for further reading.

Organizing reading for development

All of the above must now be worked into a practical way of teaching. An extended example of teaching reading for concept development should be helpful. The one offered here develops the concept *man and nature* and has been used experimentally in fifteen classrooms. The literary materials which were used in the example were pedagogically organized in this way:

THE CONCEPT OF STRUCTURE
(Relating Man and Nature)

How structure comes into being from relation. Developing (structuring) the concept *man and nature.*

A. First Subset of Cases

  1. Carl Sandburg   *The Harbor*
  2. Walt Whitman   *When I Heard the Learned Astronomer*
  3. Thomas Wolfe   *Look Homeward, Angel* (passage)
  Emerson   *Rhodora* (could be added)

  (Emerging meaning or generalization: nature is friendly to man.)

  Essay assignment: How can one justify the above as a subset?

B. Second Subset of Cases

  4. John Keats   *When I Have Fears That I May Cease To Be*
  5. Herman Melville   *Moby Dick* (passage)
  6. Eleanor Wiley   *Sea Lullaby*

  (Emerging meaning or generalization: nature is indifferent or hostile to man.)

  Attempted synthesis of the first two sets.

  Essay assignment: How I would resolve the two sets (250 words).

C. Third Subset of Cases

  7. Stephen Spender   *The Express*
  8. Aldous Huxley   *Time and the Machine*
  9. Edith Sitwell   *Dirge for the New Sunrise*
  10. Old Testament   *Book of Job* (passage)

  (Emerging meaning or generalization: man conquers nature for his own ends and turns the power on himself.)

  Essay assignment: Trial synthesis of all three sets.

D. Present new aspects of the concept nature: nature is also *in* man.

  11. Lincoln Barrett   *Universe and Dr. Einstein* (passage)
  12. de Chardin   *Phenomenon of Man* (passage)

  Essay assignment: How I now look at nature.

E. Test

13.	Stephens	*The Shell*
14.	Masefield	*Sea Fever*
15.	Turner	*Romance*
16.	Yeats	*The Lake Isle of Innisfree*
17.	Carman	*A Vagabond Song*

(All the above items in the test, save one, have a nostalgic expectancy of being close to nature.)

The final test entails two tasks:

a. How structure the five poems?

b. How relate this structure to the already-made synthesis of the preceding three subsets?

The above 17 works are the materials of instruction as organized and as serially presented to the pupils for the purpose of teaching the strategies of discovery and the invention of structure in the development of the concept *man and nature*. The reader should constantly keep in mind that the pupils never knew what poem was coming next or what relation it had to the preceding poem. The suggested generalizations were for the teachers, never for the pupils. The pupils had to discover the subsets for themselves. The above teaching outline, thus, was not a course syllabus given to the pupils. What was provided them will be explained in detail later.

Each poem and passage was given one at a time by the teacher, and each poem was analyzed and interpreted as a particular kind of entity in relation to other subsequent poems (entities). With two instances at hand, a class or generalization (subset) is beginning to form and is being modified as each new poem (instance) is encountered. The concept is gradually unfolding as more data (more poems) are presented. In our model, except for the choosing of the instances, every bit of the process continues by act of pupil discovery. The student must discover the meaning of each poem as instance; he must tie the meanings of several poems together tentatively by a generalization (subset), and then, in like manner, he must create other subsets, depending on the meaning he gives to the next instances; he next must relate groupings of poems to other groups of poems (subsets) at a different level of abstraction; and finally he must relate these abstractions to arrive at a provisional interpretation of the concept we set for him to investigate. In time he should learn the strategies of relating single poems, relating groups of poems, and relating abstractions. And it goes without saying that he should eventually know what the act of relating involves. Thus, out of dealing with a progression of instances, there results a comprehensive, panoramic structure on three levels of abstraction.

Reading as structuring

87

To accomplish this task, we provide a suggested "Guide for Pupils," which may serve to reveal indirectly to the teacher how the reading of these works enters into a method for teaching a logical process. This creative guide to help the pupils develop the concept *man and nature* was used by 10 English teachers to teach 250 pupils for a period of four weeks. All the teachers were especially trained in graduate school for a semester in concept development. But most of the teachers, although they faithfully followed the logical demand of the process, varied widely in their use of pupil-to-pupil interaction, in literary analysis, in the use of affective response, in the recourse to syntax and rhetoric, and in the appeal to pupil experience.

As illustrated here, the logical devices provided for the pupils at first may appear formal and mechanical to the average English teacher. Our use of the multiple-choice device is not to measure comprehension or to prestructure the thought as in a syllabus, but to galvanize thought and to lead to the discussion of thought—what to join, what to separate, what to discard or revise—all in the manner of Diedrich's *Critical Thinking* (1955). Our use of diagrams and the graphic analysis of a thinking process is not an occasion to dry out the poem but to work up an encounter with conflicting values. The following is a description of the affective outcome:

> Whenever youth asks "Who Am I?" or "What Does This Mean?" they are inviting a cognitive exploration; they are asking to go beyond the sock of confrontation. Structuring thought, we found, is an imperative need of youth—whether dull, average, or bright, advantaged or disadvantaged, whether "terminal" or college-bound.
>
> As proof of this need, we were amazed that motivation and interest were the least of our troubles in teaching the unit on nature to four hundred students in six schools, with different social climates and ten teachers varying in personality and style. Students of ordinary intelligence, in middle groupings, became as excited over a cognitive encounter such as "in which category to place a poem" as they would in some typical boy-girl relations unit.
>
> For instance, the encounter with the Keats sonnet literally upset many students, coming as it did after their first invented category "nature as friendly"; and Wylie's "Sea Lullaby" simply shook others; while with Sitwell's poem the students, now having something (a self-created structure) to bring to the poem, argued vehemently among themselves when they saw man more ferocious to his own kind than the vultures in *Moby Dick* or Wylie's *Strangler Sea*. That such interest could be sparked by trying to reconcile cases to a structure was due to the fact, we believe, that first we let students read every work organically for itself, as an art form, for all the "life" it possessed, before we had students try to place it in a developing structure of a concept like "nature." The poem did not exist for the structure; the reverse often happened: the poem was reread again and again for more meaning while it was being weighed for a tentatively developing category. (Henry, 1968, p. 1304)

The 15 teachers involved in the experiment of teaching reading by concept development all agreed that a launching of the unit was necessary: a reading readiness for the adventure into the concept *man and nature.* Something of this sort came into being. The following material was a handout to the pupils as a study guide. Notice how greatly it differs from the usual preplanned syllabus or unit of study and from the usual rational course outline.

A guide for pupils in concept development

HOW TO BUILD A STRUCTURE OF IDEAS
(Material for the pupil)

Let us now put our experience with the four forms of relation to work by studying the joining of two large, abstract ideas—man and nature. We will inquire into the meaning of *and* as we bring the idea *man* and the idea *nature* together for joining. We might begin by asking why men in the past have turned to nature to guide them, or have thought themselves related to nature or what use they have made of nature to interpret their own humanity. As we have observed in former selections, one poet claimed to "converse" with nature; another debated whether to shut himself tightly away from nature; still another had memories of it to live by; and another found grief sensitizing him toward nature; and lastly, two poets extracted an element from nature for our meditation—one, the idea of *gold*; the other, the idea of *standing and staring.* Could you make a case for man *or* nature instead of man *and* nature? Is nature larger than man?

In order to warm you up for our investigation of man and nature, you might try discussing with your classmates and your teacher whatever sparks fly off as you run through the questions below:

1. Is it natural for man to make fire sirens?
2. Is a siren as natural as a waterfall?
3. Is man as natural to the earth as is a tree?
4. Is it natural for a man to be a man in the way it is natural for a tree to be a tree? (Watch this one.)
5. Is it as natural for a man to think as it is for him to eat?
6. If it is natural for man to think and to create, then are the results of this thinking and creating a beautiful part of nature? Is, therefore, an atomic bomb natural? Is pollution natural?
   Is nature beautiful?
   Is the clay more natural than a vase?
   Is a painting natural?

Is painting more natural the more it looks like nature—say, a real tree?

Is it natural for men to communicate by smoke signals, tom-toms, sirens, or bells?

Is it natural for a man to enjoy waves or listen with delight to rustling leaves?

Is it natural for a man to talk with other men?

Is it natural for a waterfall or for leaves to talk to men?

Is it natural to love? To hate? To murder?

Is an Indian more of nature than a white man?

What does *close to nature* mean?

7. Are cities natural?

8. Is man good when he imitates nature? Does nature teach man lessons?

After going through the following experience of relating man and nature (which should take several weeks), we will return to this page of questions to see how you then respond to and use the idea of nature.

STRUCTURING A SET OF EXPERIENCES WITH NATURE
(For the pupil)

Bull sessions and an informal exchange of ideas in class often help us get a better hold on an idea. But an idea also grows and expands as we look at its place inside a pattern. Therefore, a class discussion is not very fruitful unless the discussion leads to a structuring of our ideas, not as final truth, but as a means of discussion in future daily classes. Suppose, as we start, there is no pattern available, and we must build our own as we go along. It would be like journeying into an unknown land without a map.

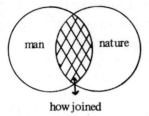

how joined

As we join and separate and negate, we must build a structure of ideas. In other words, we wish to pile and sort, but we have little or no notion of what kind of piles or what number of piles to make and what there is at hand to put into the piles. This kind of thinking is called creative thinking, or sometimes, if it is done within a situation, problematic thinking. In the following section, we will become more aware of this kind of thinking as we are confronted with an unexplored region of thought and a succession of unsorted ideas.

You are going to observe how each of three men has thought about himself in relation to nature, and then you will work the resulting ideas into a pattern.

The Harbor

Passing through huddled and ugly walls
By doorways where women
Looked from their hunger-deep eyes,
Haunted with shadows of hunger-hands,
Out from the huddled and ugly walls,
I came sudden, at the city's edge,
On a burst of lake,
Long lake waves breaking under the sun
On a spray-flung curve of shore;
And a fluttering storm of gulls,
Masses of great gray wings
And flying white bellies
Veering and wheeling free in the open.

— Carl Sandburg

1. What two main ideas are brought together? Defend your choice.
   a. passing and fluttering
   b. passing and came
   c. ugly walls and burst of lake
   d. women and gulls
   e. huddled walls and freedom of nature
   f. huddled and ugly

2. What would a still larger bringing together be?
   a. man or nature
   b. man and nature
   c. dock life and bird life
   d. nature and a man's idea of nature

3. Interpret these figures:

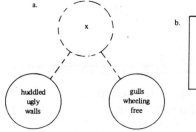

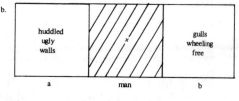

4. What is the *I* saying?
   a. Here is bad city life, and there is good free nature.
   b. Here dock life is not free, and a short distance away is free and open life.
   c. Here mankind is unnatural, and there is nature pure in itself.
   d. Here is a woman degraded and thinking of the burst of joy so close to her.
   e. Here are two sharply contrasting sensations.

5. Do you think the *I* is the poet himself? From the poem *only,* what can you safely say the speaker is like?

6. Does the poem imply:
   a. Nature (wheeling free) is a kind of norm for man's freedom.
   b. Nature (wheeling free) might be a norm for man's being natural.
   c. What a pity man cannot be natural in the way gulls are!
   d. Mankind cannot attain the freedom of the gulls.
   e. Nature can teach man how to live.
   f. Another view?

7. Which to you is the best meaning of the poem?
   a. To imitate nature is to live more naturally.
   b. To look upon nature does not make any favorable changes in the *huddled and ugly walls.*
   c. If only the dock be made as natural to man as the lake is to the gulls.

8. In what way does the phrase *burst of lake* unite man and nature? Where *is* the *burst*? Does the word *huddled* belong to the street and *free* belong to nature?

9. How does the *I* relate himself to nature? Could we as a class decide what the speaker's idea of nature is?

ANOTHER MAN'S EXPERIENCE WITH NATURE

Keeping the first speaker's view of nature in mind, let us try to put ourselves in another man's place, this time under the stars, and watch—perhaps feel—his reaction to nature.

Teaching reading as concept development

When I Heard the Learned Astronomer

When I heard the learn'd astronomer
When the proofs, the figures, were ranged in columns before me,
When I was shown the charts and diagrams, to add, divide and measure
    them,
When I sitting heard the astronomer where he lectured with much
    applause in the lecture room,
How soon unaccountable I became tired and sick,
Till rising and gliding out I wander'd off by myself,
In the mystical moist night-air, and from time to time,
Look'd up in perfect silence at the stars.

                        — Walt Whitman

1. Which of these joinings do you think shows how the ideas are put together?
    a. Here was a dry, boring lecture, and I became sick and tired of it.
    b. Here was a dry, boring lecture, and I went outdoors for relief.
    c. Here was a man displaying great learning, but I did not think he knew it all.
    d. I appreciated the marvelous knowledge the astronomer had, but I found it inadequate when I faced the stars.
    e. I learned a great deal about stars from the astronomer, and I now appreciate them all the more.
    f. I grew weary of a systematic knowledge of the universe, and I decided awe is a way to understanding, too.

2. There are two ways of learning about nature, according to this poem. Fill in the circles. (Remember your previous work with these diagrams. Your teacher will help you interpret them.)

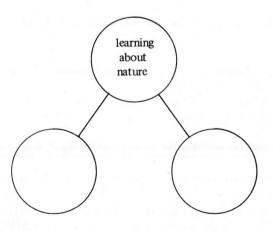

3. After reading this poem again, which of these diagrams would you defend?

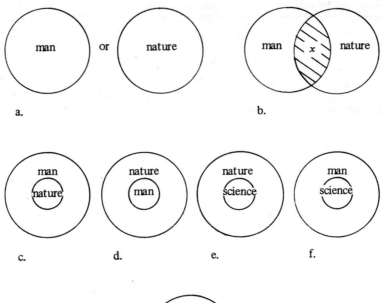

a.   b.

c.   d.   e.   f.

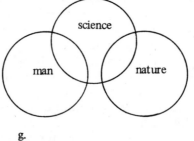

g.

4. Can man look upon himself and nature at the same time? In what way?

5. We will first discuss each of these and then select the one you think the poem means:
   a. There are some things science can never know.
   b. When we know a great deal of something the awe of it vanishes.
   c. The more we know of the stars the more wonderful they become.
   d. Man's awe really arises when he doesn't know enough about nature.
   e. Science should be aware of its own limitations.

Teaching reading as concept development

6. Prepare a short written or oral paragraph on any two of these:
   a. How does the poet regard nature?
   b. How does the poet regard himself?
   c. To what extent do you agree or disagree with the poet in light of your own idea of nature?
   d. Why are the words *unaccountable, perfect, mystical* used? Do they belong to nature?

For reflection. In "The Harbor" there is a literal joining of two parts of a harbor: the docks and the open water. In "The Learned Astronomer," there is a literal joining of a lecture and a look at the heavens. In each case, the literal joining was brought about because the poet had a purpose for doing so. The author's purpose in each poem is to reveal his feelings toward the nature of the joining.

What do the two responses have in common? What difference exists, however, in spite of their having something in common?

A THIRD EXPERIENCE WITH NATURE

We move now to a young man's use of nature to work our a nerve-racking situation—being jilted by his very first love. This experience may shed somewhat different light on our developing idea of man and nature.

LOOK HOMEWARD, ANGEL

There was another page. Weakened and relaxed from his excitement, he looked at it. There he found, almost illegibly written, but at last in her own speech, as if leaping out from the careful aimlessness of her letter, this note:

July 4

Richard came yesterday. He is twenty-five, works in Norfolk. I've been engaged to him almost a year. We're going off quietly to Norfolk tomorrow and get married. My dear! My dear! I couldn't tell you! I tried to, but couldn't. I didn't want to lie. Everything else was true. I meant all I said. If you hadn't been so young, but what is the use of saying that? Try to forgive me, but please don't forget me. Good-by and God bless you. Oh, my darling, it was heaven! I shall never forget you.

When he had finished the letter, he reread it, slowly and carefully. Then he folded it, put it in his inner breast-pocket, and leaving Dixieland, walked for forty minutes, until he came up in the gap over the town again. It was sunset. The sun's vast rim, blood-red, rested upon the western earth, in a great field of murky pollen. It sank beyond the western ranges. The clear sweet air was washed with gold and pearl. The vast hills melted into purple solitudes: they were like Canaan and rich grapes. The motors of cove people toiled up around the horse-shoe of the road. Dusk came. The bright winking lights in the town went up. Darkness melted over the town like dew: it washed out all the day's distress, the harsh confusions. Low wailing sounds came faintly up from Niggertown.

And above him the proud stars flashed into heaven: there was one, so rich and low, that he could have picked it, if he had climbed the hill beyond the Jew's great house. One, like a lamp, hung low above the heads of men returning home. (O Hesperus, you bring us all good things.) One had flashed out the light that winked on him the night that Ruth lay at the feet of Boaz; and one on Queen Isolt; and one on Corinth and on Troy. It was night, vast brooding night, the mother of loneliness, that washes our stains away. He was washed in the great river of night, in the Ganges tides of redemption. His bitter wound was for the moment healed in him: he turned his face upward to the proud and tender stars, which made him a god and a grain of dust, the brother of eternal beauty and the son of death—alone, alone.

— Thomas Wolfe

1. What does the *and* between the two paragraphs bring together?
   a. It ties up the previous sentence or idea of *low wailing sounds* and *proud stars flashed.*
   b. It brings together the thought of paragraph one and paragraph two. How?
   c. What is the thought in paragraph one (in six words)? In paragraph two? How can they be joined? Why?

2. Fill in the circles

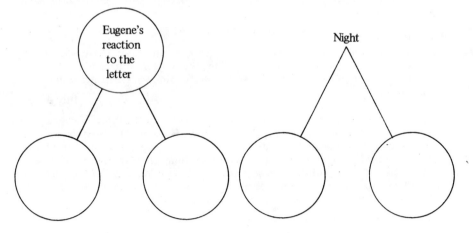

3. What does the *and* after Isolt bring together?

4. Is this *and* bringing together simultaneous time or different time?

5. What do the last two *and's* bring together?
   a. Eugene and (a god and a grain of dust)
   b. Eugene and (a brother of eternal beauty and a son of death)

6. From the text, which of these are true?
   a. Looking down and a grain of dust
   b. Looking up and a grain of dust
   c. Looking down and a son of death
   d. Looking down and a brother of beauty
   e. Looking up and a brother of beauty
   f. Looking up and a son of death
   g. Looking up and a god
   h. Looking down and a god

7. Fill in the circles

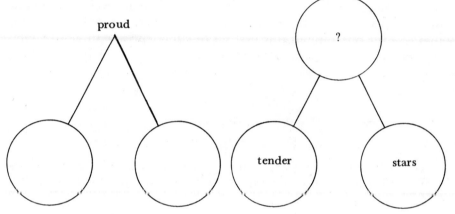

proud

tender   stars

8. What is the force of *alone*?

Here there is a most dramatic joining of seeming opposites—down in the valley, up among the stars. Eugene's emotion or tension holds the two together. The remarkable joining of *proud* and *tender, a god* and *a grain of dust,* is not strictly a logical one, but a joining by mood. How is this possible?

What would you say is the youth's attitude toward nature? What would it have in common with the two previous attitudes? Does it add something to our understanding that the others do not?

So far, we have tried to get ourselves inside three experiences with nature. Each situation was quite different from the others. What can we say we learned from these experiences about how three men related themselves to nature? What kind of technique for joining these three experiences do we have? From your past dealing with the act of joining, you will recall that our problem may look like this:

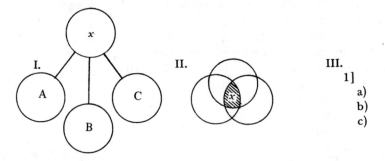

To the teacher. In our experiment in concept development each of the 15 classes, with the aid of their teacher, created a structure that was the outcome of this first set of experiences with nature. One is given below as one class framed it.

CHART 1

Structuring Subset I

The Possible Pattern for All Three Instances

I All three men go to nature to find in it a relief or a satisfaction after experiencing something that worried them within the society of man.
   A. Nature recalls history and eternal time (Wolfe).
   B. Nature highlights the evil of society by being pure (Sandburg).
   C. Nature supplements the knowledge gained by the intellect (Whitman).

II Nature seems to supply some lack in man.
   A. The presumptions of man (Whitman).
   B. The hurt feelings of man (Wolfe).
   C. The social restrictions on man (Sandburg).

III Nature is larger than man.
   A. Deeper than reason (Whitman).
   B. Longer than one's life or any present woe (Wolfe).
   C. More free and spontaneous (Sandburg).

IV Nature elevates man.
   A. Through mystical union (Whitman).
   B. By inspiring us (Sandburg).
   C. By bringing all time before us (Wolfe).

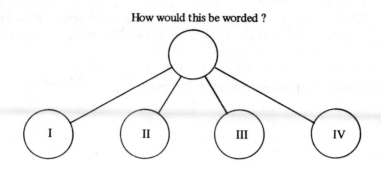

How would this be worded ?

I   II   III   IV

THREE MORE EXPERIENCES WITH NATURE

You have now sketched in a structure of ideas based on three experiences with nature. Your structure of ideas is tentative, of course, because, limited to only a few cases, it could hardly be called final. As you move through the next set of three experiences, note the challenge each new experience presents to your previously built structure.

Our first poem reveals a young man facing the heavens and the sea alone, much like Eugene Gant in *Look Homeward, Angel* standing on the hill alone.

When I Have Fears That I May Cease To Be*

When I have fears that I may cease to be
Before my pen has glean'd my teeming brain,
Before high-piled books, in charact'ry,
Hold like full garners the full-ripen'd grain;
When I behold, upon the night's starr'd face,
Huge cloudy symbols of a high romance,
And feel that I may never live to trace
Their shadows, with the magic hand of chance;
And when I feel, fair creature of an hour!
That I shall never look upon thee more,
Never have relish in the faery power
Of unreflecting love;—then on the shore
Of the wide world I stand alone, and think,
Till Love and Fame to nothingness do sink.

— John Keats

1. Which is the best meaning of what the poet is saying?
   a. Here is a young man who has much that he wants to do and little time in which to do it.
   b. Here is a young man with three desires in mind, and he realizes he will never live long enough to carry them out.

*The poet has tuberculosis and knows he does not have long to live.

c. Here is a young man who knows that his hopes will never be fulfilled and in seeking an answer he finds no importance in them after all.

d. Your version, if one of the above does not fit.

2. This poem implies which one of these?

   a. Nature does not care about man.
   b. Why does nature deprive me of what I am capable of?
   c. Nature offers me talent, beauty, and love and then takes these from me without reason.
   d. Why strive to be somebody?
   e. Life is joyous and wonderful, and I shall never fully live it.
   f. The highest things of life are meaningless in the face of death.

3. Answer each and defend your view.

   a. The poet comments on nature's lack of an answer to his predicament.
   b. The poet condemns nature.
   c. The poet condemns himself.
   d. The poet tries to account for his predicament.
   e. The poet appeals to nature to help him.
   f. The poet reveals that no one is to blame for his situation.

4. The poet—

   a. Does he seem defeated?
   b. Has he lost faith?
   c. Has he made peace with life?
   d. Does thought help him?
   e. Does he find life meaningless?
   f. Does he resign himself to be nothing?
   g. Has he won something beyond this world?

In the three poems of the first set, each man, as you have indicated, took a somewhat large, comforting, inspirational view from nature. What did Keats discover in nature? Did he lack or add something that the other three had? Is his situation more desperate than the others? Is it more desperate than Eugene's?

Does this poem bring something new to our search to understand man's relation to nature? Can it be reconciled to our first-created pattern as a fourth case? Write a theme in 400 words explaining how this poem adds an interpretation of nature different from the other three; or explain how it can logically fit into the first structure.

At this stage you might suggest a plausible bridge between your present structure and this particular poem. What would such a bridge be like? For instance, can we take what we now know—that is, the structure we have created—and relate it to the something new in this poem, especially if this new poem does not seem to fit? We mean, *Can we find a logical place for it?* Can we keep our original pattern but alter it somewhat to find a place for the new experience Keats went through? We might think of our presently created structure as a mainland and the new idea in Keats' poem as an island. How can we bridge the two? Should we erect a tentative bridge and see how well the gap can be arched? We might also wait, temporarily, to see what our next experience with nature brings forth.

Note to the reader: The accompanying analysis (Chart 2) is an attempt to explain what is logically taking place when the pupils are confronted with a fourth case, after their making the first structure.

CHART 2
A MODEL FOR HYPOTHETICAL THINKING
WITHIN THE INVENTION OF STRUCTURE
(For Students)

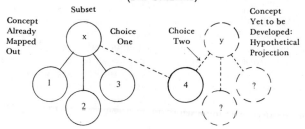

Task: *What to do with the instance 4?*
  Heavy lines = structure already framed
  Broken lines =   (1) two possible choices in reference to x.
                   (2) temporarily place it in either and wait for the next instance
                   (3) wait for the next instance, combine it or not with 4 and relate
                        it to x or create y.
  A way to test the placing of the instance:
                   (1) Does it have an attribute as criterial as those that formed
                        structure x?
                   (2) Is there an attribute so different from these that it violates x?
                   (3) Notice that the full meaning of 4 will not be known until we
                        decide where to place it.

(For Teachers)
Our modification of Bruner's analysis of a "mental" process in *A Study of Thinking*, (p. 233):
  1. An array of instances (Cases 1, 2, 3, 4, etc.).
  2. Tentative prediction of each case to fall into a subset, a decision to be made
     (what to do with case 4?).
  3. Validation of the decision (tentative?).
  4. Each decision provides potential information and includes or reduces the
     number of attributes to be handled.
  5. Sequence of decisions to discover valid clues—a strategy embodying certain
     objectives. What could be the nature of y?
  6. Consequences are set in motion by the decision. A follow-through by testing
     obtained results and/or by exploring the emerging new structure of relations,
     y, as distinct from x.

If psychologically the mind works like the above when confronted with elements serially, how can this process be developed, refined, accelerated, or improved? In what way does instruction help? How can this improvement be measured? This is the heart of the inquiry and provides us with a base for our hypothesis.

From our first set of three experiences we have created a pattern of ideas concerning man and nature. Then the Keats' experience posed a problem: how to work it into our emerging structure? This poem complicates our tidy structure. As you preceed to the next experience below, does it and the Keats' poem have more in common than they have with the first set? Determine what they do have in common. Could this new common idea be harmonized with the common idea running through the first set of three? Do you now sense a new kind of overall structure developing? Let's turn to this second experience with nature and observe how it influences our evolving structure of ideas about man and nature.

The Funeral
from *Moby Dick*
(Chapter 69)

Haul in the chains! Let the carcass go astern!

The vast tackles have now done their duty. The peeled white body of the beheaded whale flashes like a marble sepulchre; though changed in hue, it has not perceptibly lost anything in bulk. It is still colossal. Slowly it floats more and more away, the water round it torn and splashed by the insatiate sharks, and the air above vexed with rapacious flights of screaming fowls, whose beaks are like so many insulting poniards in the whale. The vast white headless phantom floats further and further from the ship, and every rod that it so floats, what seem square roods of sharks and cubic roods of fowls, augment the murderous din. For hours and hours from the almost stationary ship that hideous sight is seen. Beneath the unclouded and mild azure sky, upon the fair face of the pleasant sea, wafted by the joyous breezes, that great mass of death floats on and on, till lost in infinite perspectives.

There's a most doleful and most mocking funeral! The sea-vultures all in pious mourning, the air-sharks all punctiliously in black or speckled. In life but few of them would have helped the whale, I ween, if peradventure he had needed it; but upon the banquet of his funeral they most piously do pounce. Oh, horrible vulturism of earth! from which not the mightiest whale is free.

— Herman Melville

1. What does the passage say?
   a. All things die, even lords of the earth.
   b. There is no cooperation in nature.
   c. Calm, pleasant sea and hulk of death.
   d. Nature is a vast game of tooth and claw.

2. The writer's view of nature. Which is true?
   a. He is not deliberately going to nature to seek some answer from her.

b. He is a spectator and objectively comes to a conclusion about nature.
c. Nature is a nonmoral awesome interplay or give and take beyond good and evil.
d. This magnificent horror tells man that nature does not need him.
e. This man accepts nature as an enemy.

3. By implication, which is true?
   a. A demon rather than a god runs the universe.
   b. Man must fight nature with all the means at his command.
   c. It is foolish to ask questions of nature.
   d. In tackling nature as a foe man sees his own nature better.

As a class, with the help of your teacher, you might make a tentative structure to contain these two experiences with nature. What would this structure be like? Does it fit into the first structure in any way? After roughly sketching in the hybrid structure, let's go on to a third experience.

Sea Lullaby

The old moon is tarnished
With smoke of the flood,
The dead leaves are varnished
With color like blood,

A treacherous smiler
With teeth white as mild,
A savage beguiler
In sheathings of sild,

The sea creeps to pillage,
She leaps on her prey;
A child of the village
Was murdered today.

She came up to meet him
In a smooth golden cloak
She choked him and beat him
To death, for a joke.

Her bright locks were tangled,
She shouted for joy,
With one hand she strangled
A strong little boy.

Now in silence she lingers
Beside him all night
To wash her long fingers
In silvery light.

— Elinor Wylie

1. Developing the thought:
   a. What is the reason for calling this poem a lullaby?
   b. Why does the poet carefully summon up beautiful images before us?
   c. Does the absence of *ands* in this poem mean that there is no fundamental joining of two ideas?
   d. What ideas are joined?

2. What is the poem saying?
   a. Nature is beautiful but treacherous.
   b. Nature has no conscience.
   c. The writer does not go to nature for relief from trouble.
   d. The writer is a spectator and related just what she sees.

3. By implication, which is true?
   a. The laws of nature should not be confused with nature's beauty.
   b. The writer is really passing judgment on nature.
   c. Nature is indifferent to man.
   d. If man imitates nature, we would all be murderers.

4. What is *x*?

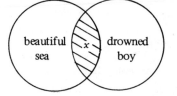

LOOKING FOR PATTERN OR STRUCTURE

1. What do the poem "Sea Lullaby" and the passage from *Moby Dick* ("Funeral") have in common?

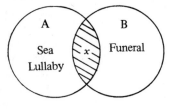

2. How do these two attitudes toward nature differ from "When I Have Fears"? What would be *x*?

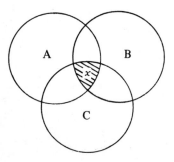

Teaching reading as concept development

What kind of structure could we work out for *x*?

Create, if you can, a structure for this second set of experiences; put it in lattice form, then into an outline.

Note to the reader: This same class working in groups, after much discussion and revision, decided that the next three experiences form a second set that can be structured in this way (Chart 3).

CHART 3
Structuring Subset II

I.   Nature is indifferent to man's life (Keats).
  A.   It cares nothing about the goals of man (fame or love).
  B.   It cares not whether man fulfills himself.
  C.   There is no end toward which nature strives.

II. Nature provides no norm or model for man to live by (Melville).
  A.   Neither competition nor cooperation among men is favored by nature.
  B.   It can form no basis for moral conduct.
  C.   Man needs nature (whale) but nature does not need man.
  D.   Natural law and moral law are distinct.

III. Nature is hostile and treacherous to man (Wylie).
  A.   Man must protect himself against nature.
  B.   The beauty of nature gives no hope to man.
  C.   Man is not nature's favorite child.

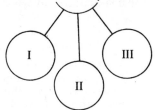

There is no basic moral order in the universe outside the society of man.

Now you have a kind of problem you have not encountered so far. You have two structures. Can you work out some kind of pattern that would reconcile or unite the two different structures that you now have before you? Is it possible to join them by some larger third idea (*and*), or are they fundamentally disjunctive (*or*)? As you see it, write out your views about the troubles you are encountering in the joining of the two structures.

SEVERAL MORE EXPERIENCES WITH NATURE

At the end of the first three poems you made a tentative structure of how some men have related themselves to nature. The second set of experiences led you to create a different structure. Now you have to work out a pattern from these two structures to serve you to analyze any additional cases that may come your way. In what important way do we have to change our original pattern to accommodate the second set of cases? Or, would some generalization, more highly abstract, be a way of uniting the two structures? The task now seems to be this:

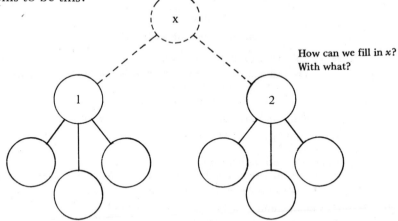

How can we fill in x? With what?

Suppose we let the dotted part lie empty for a while. We can still use the partly completed structure as if it were whole, to help us interpret some other cases of men looking at nature or relating themselves to it. The following poem introduces another relationship. Try to point out what it is and speculate on what it may do to our latest partially complete working pattern.

The Express

After the first powerful plain manifesto
The black statement of pistons, without more fuss
But gliding like a queen, she leaves the station.
Without bowing and with restrained unconcern
She passes the houses which humbly crowd outside,
The gasworks and at last the heavy page
Of death, printed by gravestones in the cemetery.
Beyond the town there lies the open country
Where, gathering speed, she acquires mystery,
The luminous self-possession of ships on ocean.
It is now she begins to sing—at first quite low
Then loud, and at last with a jazzy madness—
The song of her whistle screaming at curves,
Of deafening tunnels, brakes, innumerable bolts.
And always light, aerial, underneath
Goes the elate meter of her wheels.
Steaming through metal landscape on her lines
She plunges new eras of wild happiness

Teaching reading as concept development

Where speed throws up strange shapes, broad curves
And parallels clean like the steel of guns.
At last, further than Edinburgh or Rome,
Beyond the crest of the world, she reaches night
Where only a low streamline brightness
Of phosphorus on the tossing hills is white.
Ah, like a comet through flames she moves entranced
Wrapt in her music no bird song, no, nor bough
Breaking with honey buds, shall ever equal.

— Stephen Spender

1. What does the poem mean?
   a. Man is a creator of machines that can conquer nature.
   b. What man makes is as poetic as anything nature can create.
   c. Nature can be bent to the needs of man.
   d. Here is a mechanical invention that opens up to man many new experiences with nature.

2. From the following statements, show that more can be implied from the meaning of the poem.
   a. Man is rapidly becoming as powerful as nature.
   b. Being a conqueror, man no longer needs to go to nature for consolation as in Set I.
   c. Man can look with scorn on the unfriendliness of nature as in Set II.
   d. The machine is of more help to man than is nature.

How would you seek *x* in this relationship?

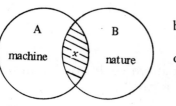

Here is a cue to help your thinking:

a. Only man can create a machine, not nature.

b. Biologically, man is *in* nature, is not himself a machine.

c. We now have an interesting complication: Around which two would you put parentheses—man and machine and nature?

If you are having trouble framing a pattern for *x*, maybe this essay will shed some light on the relation between *A* and *B*.

From **Time and the Machine**

This brings us to a seeming paradox. Acutely aware of the smallest constituent particles of time—of time, as measured by clockwork and train arrivals and the revolutions of machines—industrialized man has to a great extent lost the old awareness of time in its larger division. The time of which we have knowledge is artificial, machine-made time. Of natural, cosmic time, as it is measured out by sun and moon, we are for the most part almost wholly unconscious. Preindustrial people know time in its daily, monthly, and seasonal rhythms. They are aware of sunrise, noon, and sunset; of the full moon and the new; of equinox and solstice; of spring and summer, autumn and winter. All the old religions have insisted on this daily and seasonal rhythm. Preindustrial man was never allowed to forget the majestic movement of cosmic time.

Industrialism and urbanism have changed all this. One can live and work in a town without being aware of the daily march of the sun across the sky; without ever seeing the moon and stars. Broadway, The Piccadilly, are our Milky Way; our constellations are outlined in neon tubes. Even changes of season affect the townsman very little. He is the inhabitant of an artificial universe that is, to a great extent, walled off from the world of nature. Outside the walls, time is cosmic and moves with the motion of sun and stars. Within, it is an affair of revolving wheels and is measured in seconds and minutes—at its longest, in eight-hour days and six-day weeks. We have a new consciousness; but it has been purchased at the expense of the old consciousness.

— Aldous Huxley

1. What is Huxley saying?
   a. Man, by his machines, is creating a time different from the time of nature.
   b. The time that man is creating is not so good for man as is the time of nature.
   c. The time man creates is also changing man himself.
   d. Man's closeness to nature is being broken.

Notice the new relationship:

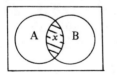

What pattern could you invent for x in this case?

A = man-made time

B = nature's time

Exercise. Write in four hundred words what you think x is. Also, how valid is this case if the relation were expressed by *or*, machine or nature? Is the issue *or* or *and*?

Let us move, now, to a new experience.

Teaching reading as concept development

From **Dirge for the New Sunrise***

Fifteen minutes past eight o'clock on the morning of
Monday the sixth of August 1945.

There was a morning when the Holy Light
Was young. The beautiful First Creature came
To our water-springs, and thought us without blame.
Our hearts seemed safe in our breasts and sang to the Light—
The marrow in the bone
We dreamed was safe. . . the blood in the veins, the sap in the tree
Were springs of Deity.

But I saw the little Ant-men as they ran
Carrying the world's weight of the world's filth
And the filth in the heart of Man—
Compressed till those lusts and greeds had a greater heat
    than that of the Sun.

And the ray from that heat came soundless, shook the sky
As if in search of food, and squeezed the stems
Of all that grows on the earth till they were dry
—and drank the marrow of the bone:
The eyes that saw, the lips that kissed, are gone
Or black as thunder lie and grin at the murdered Sun.

The living blind and seeing dead together lie
As if in love. . . There was no more hating then,
And no more love: Gone is the heart of Man.

— Edith Sitwell

1. Which of these is the poet saying?
   a. The machine man devised to conquer nature has been used
      against himself.
   b. Nothing in nature, including the nature in man—blood and
      marrow—can escape the destructive power of man's in-
      ventions.
   c. Splitting the atom has put a god-like amount of nature's
      energy at the command of man.
   d. The more man subdues nature, the greater he becomes as a
      human being.

2. In light of our last three cases which of these is likely to happen?
   a. As man increasingly dominates nature, man will not go to
      nature for mystical union as in "The Learned Astron-
      omer."
   b. As man uses the earth with his new knowledge, he need not
      care about nature's "vulturism" as in Melville.

*This poem refers to the explosion of the first atomic bomb.

c. As man's machines are perfected, he will be more awed by his own creations (Brooklyn Bridge, a missile to Mars, the submarine "Polaris") than overawed by a sunrise, as in "The Harbor."

d. Man will rely less and less on nature for spiritual strength.

TOWARD STRUCTURING THESE NEW EXPERIENCES
(meaning of x)

What is x?

a. Man's invention of the machine has altered his view of nature?

b. Man's invention of the machine has altered nature herself?

c. Man has a power to command that rivals that of nature's.

As man conquers space, he has a different image of himself.

1. Man will turn away from nature in his effort to discern his own destiny.

a. It will not be necessary to go to nature to find a guide to life.

b. Man is slowly becoming indifferent to the Christmas tree, Easter, harvest home, and May Day.

New questions before man in this century:

1. Is there a foreboding that man will not use his power over nature wisely?

2. Where will man find the goals to direct the power he wrings from nature?

3. In conquering nature is man ruining it and himself?

We now have three structures of three ideas (concepts of nature). How can these complex structures be joined? We must build a structure of several overarching levels, something like this:

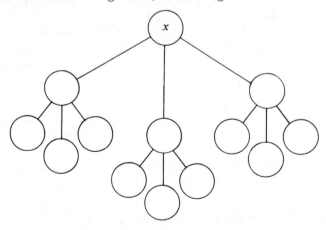

Teaching reading as concept development

Just as we had to discover a common ground for three separate, single experiences—that is, create a "set"—on three separate occasions, so we must now discover a common ground for the three structures. This task requires a new higher level of abstraction. As a class let us try our hand at inventing a super-structure of all the poems and passages. *(Note to the reader. See Chart 4, page 112.)*

Suppose we now examine this large structure as a structure. Can you think of other dimensions of man and nature that need to be explored? Would there be the possibility of a new set? What reading needs to be done to develop this new dimension?

Now that we have come to the school end of our study of the relation between man and nature, what have we learned? At no place along the line of our developing knowledge did we indicate that you were dealing with final relations or final truth. Several times along the way you were forced to modify a structure that seemed to fall short of explaining a new case. The structure that you have now achieved as you close the study is as good as you could make it, given the sets of cases that came before you and the method of reasoning at your command. This structure can be used well in dealing with future cases. It is, of course, tentative and incomplete, yet it can help yield good meanings as you come upon unknown cases.

As we live our lives, our limited selves are not presented with the full range of cases existing at any one time; in addition, as time or history goes on, man brings into being new relations with nature not formerly available to us. It may well be that next week either in some course in school or at church or during personal reading you will encounter a view of nature that was not included in this study. All we can say is that you will have to incorporate this island of ideas into the mainland of ideas you have now forged. As you live, new islands will pop up for absorption into your main body of belief, until after 20 years or so, you may have a completely restructured pattern of belief about man and nature. This reorganization of one's pattern of ideas is what is generally meant by growing wiser.

What, then, have you learned? One, you have acquired some ideas about man and nature and have put them, as best you can, into a pattern which is usually called subject matter; in other words, you have learned how subject matter is made. Two, you have learned what is meant by *relation*: that is, a form of thinking, a way of bringing things and ideas into larger patterns, a way of handling new cases, new ideas. Three, you have learned that man (this means you) never has a perfect pattern to go by at any moment of decision, and yet he must have a pattern if he is to live well.

CHART 4

HOW ONE CLASS CREATED A STRUCTURE OF MAN AND NATURE

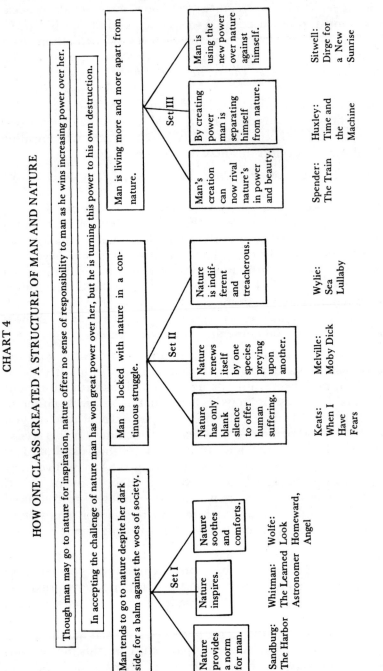

Though man may go to nature for inspiration, nature offers no sense of responsibility to man as he wins increasing power over her.

In accepting the challenge of nature man has won great power over her, but he is turning this power to his own destruction.

Man tends to go to nature despite her dark side, for a balm against the woes of society.

Set I

Nature provides a norm for man.

Nature inspires.

Nature soothes and comforts.

Sandburg: The Harbor

Whitman: The Learned Astronomer

Wolfe: Look Homeward, Angel

Man is locked with nature in a continuous struggle.

Set II

Nature has only blank silence to offer human suffering.

Nature renews itself by one species preying upon another.

Nature is indifferent and treacherous.

Keats: When I Have Fears

Melville: Moby Dick

Wylie: Sea Lullaby

Man is living more and more apart from nature.

Set III

Man's creation can now rival nature's in power and beauty.

By creating power man is separating himself from nature.

Man is using the new power over nature against himself.

Spender: The Train

Huxley: Time and the Machine

Sitwell: Dirge for a New Sunrise

Notes:

The next steps would be: 1) find flaws with the structure; 2) compare with another structure; 3) examine more cases or instances. Examples: Where would you put the passage from Job in this pattern? Where would the novel *Lord of the Flies* fit in? 4) Are there other dimensions needed? 5) How does one fit a new structure into the above larger structure you have created?

Teaching reading as concept development.

Even if someone wiser than you gave you a ready-made map (pattern) to live by (one better than you could do), you would still have the problem of how to make it a part of yourself; and what would be even more difficult for you to do would be to handle several conflicting patterns, each ready-made for you and each claiming to be more complete than the others. So we are really back where we were originally—each of us must learn to use conflicting subject matter for himself in his own living. From this wide variety of cases that you have now analyzed (the actual number is much more varied), you have a bit of subject matter and a method of dealing with the relations that build subject matter; you may now do better what each human being must do cautiously yet confidently for himself all life long—relate himself to nature.

Let us imagine the future. Suppose in a month or so you hear a minister read this passage from the Book of Job in the *Old Testament,* or suppose you come upon it in your reading. How would you respond to it, now that you know what you do about man and nature?

Book of Job

The Voice (speaking as if a whirlwind: still, small, very penetrating)

Who is this that darkeneth counsel by words without knowledge?
Gird up now thy loins like a man;
For I will demand of thee, and declare thou unto me.
Where wast thou when I laid the foundations of the earth?
—Declare if thou hast understanding—
Who determined the measures thereof, if thou knowest?
Or who stretched the line upon it?
Whereupon were the foundations thereof fastened?
Or who laid the cornerstone thereof,
When the morning stars sang together,
And all the sons of God shouted for joy?
Or who shut up the sea with doors,
When I brake forth, as if it had issued out of the womb;
When I made the cloud the garment thereof,
And thick darkness a swaddling band for it,
And marked out for it my bound,
And set bars and doors,
And said, "Hitherto shalt thou come, but no further;
And here shall thy proud waves be stayed"
Hast thou commanded the morning since thy days began,
And caused the dayspring to know its place;
That it might take hold of the ends of the earth.
And the wicked be shaken out of it? (38:1-13)

Let us imagine, a year hence, reading this passage in the field of biology. Knowing the subject matter about man and nature as you do and a method of creating a pattern, make whatever comments upon it you can.

And now, finally, assume that in your scientific readings you met the previous statement. How would you bring this island into the mainland? How would you reconstruct x? Is this final? Does man's landing on the moon alter what has just been said? What do Job and de Chardin have in common? At this point, how do you relate yourself to nature?

Logical process as a source of unity in teaching reading

The above guide for students represents the fundamental way the concept Man and Nature was taught, though each of the ten teachers varied his treatment both in respect to the unpredictable pupil response to the questioning and to the kinds of language activities employed throughout. Some used panels, individual reports, committees, recordings, displays, acting out, choral speaking, extra subject matter, and especially the pupils' past experiences (from well-nigh spilled-out confession to personal anecdote)—all of these in different sequences and in creative combinations. But all teaching had in common a steady, sustained movement toward developing the concept through discovery of relation and invention of structure, both of which were deliberately arrived at by extension and levels of abstraction. The source of unity, the teachers were aware, lay in the process of logic. The pupils, too, became aware that this kind of thinking is needed in a search for larger meaning.

As the pupil matures in such structure building, we can go on to larger tasks. For there are other root concepts in American culture that can be developed in this way, so that in time the investigation of these concepts becomes, for the most part, the curriculum itself.

Such basic concepts as these may be worked up at various levels of difficulty: Law and Order (Authority), The Hero, Optimism, Success, The Machine, The Good Life, The American Dream, The West, and Idealism and Pragmatism. This creation of logical structure is not an end, for it, like the Sabbath, was made for man. We bring a larger frame to the teaching of a work: the deeper the pupil's experience of it may be, the more likely an experience may arise in future reading. (Henry, 1968, p. 248)

Conclusion

This inquiry into affective thinking is offered with a sense of pioneering inside a realm that pedagogically has not been much explored: how might elements of the new logic enter into the teaching of reading? Although Piaget and Bruner have translated into learning theory the investigations of the great logicians of the first quarter of this century and although many educators and reading specialists have been influenced by their theory of thinking, few in the language arts and few responsible for reading in our schools have examined these theories to see what they may yield for a method of teaching reading. This inquiry has tried to do that.

In most educational writing, new terms like *process, structure*, and *discovery* are rather empty of referents to specific classroom behavior. These terms, although they sound objective, have not been put into discernible teaching acts, especially in reading. This inquiry has endeavored to turn these molar terms into atomic strategies and operations.

We have offered here a way of conceiving reading as a number of logical processes instead of a list of discrete reading skills. The intent is not so much to abandon these skills as to fuse them into the logical process where they belong.

Another guiding theory throughout this book has been that the teaching of reading should aim to refine what pupils, even slow pupils, will do when they read.

Our present reading system is built largely on tests of comprehension that are often used to evaluate the progress of a whole school system. Reading education today too seldom fosters creative response to the text. Under these conditions, the modicum of response allowed the pupil is directed toward the test not the text. To extract content as measured in the testing of reading, as some reading laboratories now design tests, does not much improve a pupil's control of the logical strategies in reading. For this reason, then, this inquiry suggests the creation of tests that attempt to measure the strategies that the pupil resorts to in his reading: tests so formed that they advance the learning of how to read.

Now it may be that research will never be able to delineate the subtle progression of steps in a logical process, like joining, synthesis, induction, problem solving (which Dewey tried). So far, there is still controversy over whether there is one method of science; while the Bloom taxonomy, another attempt at steps or levels in thinking, was not used here because it seems to lack the dynamic flow of actual thought.

Perhaps the best that research can do for a long time is to determine the conditions for good thinking, which is to say, those conditions that do allow full intuitive play of the fundamental operators that are natural to all of us. But intuition, which Bruner claims is being stifled in our schools, is largely an unexpected, muse-inspired propulsion which must eventually be controlled. Yet to earn control of intuitive thought, one must first be aware of thinking—a truism not yet made integral to a method of teaching reading. For this reason, our approach is part of an exploration of how to teach such awareness of logical process through reading.

But intuition in logic is not the same as a welling up of feeling toward a text, though both intuition and feeling are spontaneous. Throughout, *Teaching Reading as Concept Development* tries to unite intuition, logic, and feeling in the act of reading. In the middle sixties a countermovement against structure, process, and form emerged, typified by terms such as *permissiveness, spontaneity, freedom, openness, heightened experience, self-expression, doing one's own thing.* The new logic that had begun to make its way into the sequential curriculum, it was charged, brought death in the classroom. Time-honored exercises in reading were declared to be joyless, unnatural, and dehumanizing—devoid of the affective side of our humanity. In the language arts, the Dartmouth Conference (1966) was a symbol of this clash. A facile way out for the teacher of reading would be some of both realms.

As a result of this counter thrust, the theory of concept development presented here is designed to show that the logic of process and the existential encounter can and should be organically taught in reading. Intellectual conflict stirs our feelings; our feelings beg for structure, what Camus calls "That nostalgia for unity."

The need for more research in reading as affective thinking

Much still needs to be done in the direction that we have explored here. As the original inquiry proceeded, there were other areas to explore or some areas to be more deeply tunneled. This constant awareness led to an identification of some investigations into concept development that presently need to be undertaken:

1. Those concerned with the teaching of reading should try to rid themselves of such phrases as *higher thinking, depth, reading for power, clear thinking,* and *measuring comprehension.* These empty abstractions do not contribute much to our communication about the teaching of reading.

2. More research should take other elements of the new logic expressly to investigate the nature of reading—the teaching of context, of abstraction, of probability and necessity, and of awareness of self-response to a text.

3. There should be a concerted attempt among those who teach reading to break up a logical process into appropriate observable behavior of the pupil. We need to know more exactly how the four operators weave in and out of our reading. Squire (1964) did something of this sort in his study of the responses of adolescents as they read; Rosenblatt did in "The Poem As Event" (1964); Erwin Steinberg, in induction (1967); Postman and Weingartner, in context of reading (1966); Ennis (1969), and Bellack (1965), in the logic of the classroom discussion over what has been read.

4. Reading for synthesis should be gone into more thoroughly, both in theory and practice. Toward this end, anthologies of reading material might be organized either around processes of thought or about levels of degree of structuring, arranged in small to large groupings. Manuals on composition, too, should reveal to teachers how to do a content analysis, not of rhetorical organization entirely, but of clues to the pupil's strategy of thinking in his reading.

5. The age-old dichotomy between reason and feeling, structure and freedom, is upon us once again as it has appeared periodically over the past centuries. Those who teach reading in our day of neoprogressive education are obligated to teach reason *in relation to* feeling—not one and then the other.

The idea of concept development presented here does not suggest that it is the *only* way to teach reading. It hopes, instead, to have delineated and clarified for the teacher those logical strategies necessary in reading for concept development.

Teaching reading as concept development

REFERENCES

Bellack, Arno A. *The Language of the Classroom.* New York: Institute of Psychological Research, Teachers College, Columbia University, 1965.

Blanshard, Brand. *The Nature of Thought,* Volume I. New York: Macmillan, 1955, 64, 128, 542.

Bloom, B. S. *Taxonomy of Educational Objectives,* Handbook I, Cognitive Domain. New York: David McKay, 1956.

Bridgman, Percy Williams. *The Way Things Are.* Cambridge, Massachusetts: Harvard University Press, 1959, 95, 169.

Broudy, Harry S. "Mastery" in B. Othanel Smith and Robert H. Ennis (Eds.), *Language and Concepts in Education.* Chicago: Rand McNally, 1961, 82.

Bruner, Jerome S., J. J. Goodnow, and G. A. Austin. *A Study of Thinking.* New York: John Wiley and Sons, 1956.

Bruner, Jerome S. *The Process of Education.* Cambridge, Massachusetts: Harvard University Press, 1960.

Burton, Dwight et al. *The Development and Testing of Approaches to the Teaching of English in the Junior High School.* Project No. H-026, U. S. Department of Health, Education, and Welfare, 1968.

Carnap, Rudolf. *The Logical Syntax of Language.* New York: Humanities Press, 1937.

Carnegie-Mellon. The Project English Center. *A Senior High School Curriculum in English for Able College-Bound Students.* New York: Barnes and Noble, 1968. (Also *Summary Report,* 1965, 65-67.)

Certner, Simon, and George H. Henry. *Short Stories for Our Times.* Boston: Houghton Mifflin, 1950.

Craig, G. Armour. "Three Poets on a Single Theme," in Edward Gordon (Ed.), *Writing and Literature in the Secondary School.* New York: Holt, Rinehart, and Winston, 1965, 284, 288, 293-294.

Curwin, Darcy. "Teaching Biography in the Secondary School," *Commission on English.* Boston: College Entrance Examination Board, 1965.

de Chardin, Pierre Teilhard. *The Phenomenon of Man.* New York: Harper and Row, 1959, 226.

Diedrich, Paul B. *Critical Thinking in Reading and Writing.* New York: Holt, Rinehart and Winston, 1955, 199-207.

Ennis, Robert H. *Logic in Teaching.* Englewood Cliffs, New Jersey: Prentice-Hall, 1969.

Evans, Bertram. "Writing and Composing," *English Journal,* January 1959.

Feidelson, Charles. "Three Views of the Human Person," in Edward Gordon (Ed.), *Writing and Literature in the Secondary School.* New York: Holt, Rinehart, and Winston, 1965, 276-277, 284.

Green, Jay E. *Comparative Classics.* New York: Noble and Noble, 1963.

Henry, George H. "The Idea of Coverage," *English Journal,* September 1965, 475-482.

Henry, George H. "Teaching Literature by Concept Development," *English Journal,* December 1968, 1297-1306.

Henry, George H. "The Unit Method: The New Logic Meets the Old," *English Journal,* March 1967, 402-406.

Henry, George H. "The Place of Logical Structures in Teaching Literature," *College English*, December 1968, 248-249.

Henry, George H., and John Brown. *An Inquiry Into the Nature of Concept Development within the Ongoing Classroom Situation*, Project Number 1487, Contract Number O.E. 2-10-128. Washington, D. C.: U. S. Office of Education, 1965.

Herbart, J. F. *Outline of Educational Doctrine* (1806). Translated by Alexis F. Lange, 1901. New York: Macmillan, 1901.

Langer, Susanne K. *An Introduction to Symbolic Logic*. New York: Dover Publications, 1953, 26-27.

Oregon Curriculum. *A Curriculum in English, Grades 7-12*. Eugene, Oregon: Curriculum Study Center, University of Oregon, 1965, 4-11.

Piaget, Jean. *Logic and Psychology*. Translated by W. Mays and F. Whitehead. New York: Basic Books, 1957, X, 39-40.

Popper, Karl R. *The Logic of Scientific Discovery*. New York: Basic Books, 1959, 421.

Postman, Neil, and Charles Weingartner. *Linguistics*. New York: Dell Publishing, 1966.

Richards, I. A. *Interpretation in Teaching*. New York: Harcourt, Brace, 1938, 294.

Rockowitz, Murray, and Milton Kaplan. *The World of Poetry*. New York: Globe Book, 1965, 435.

Rosenblatt, Louise. "The Poem as Event," *College English*, November 1964.

Russell, Bertrand, and Alfred North Whitehead. *Principia Mathematica*. Cambridge, England: Cambridge University Press, 1910, 1912, 1913.

Schwab, Joseph J. *Education and the Structure of the Disciplines*, Part One and Two, project on the Instructional Program of the Public Schools. Washington, D. C.: National Education Association, 1961.

Sochor, E. Elona. "The Nature of Critical Reading," *Critical Reading*. Champaign, Illinois: National Council of Teachers of English, 1959.

Squire, James. *The Responses of Adolescents*, Research Monograph No. 2. Champaign, Illinois: National Council of Teachers of English, 1964.

Steinberg, Erwin R. et al. *The Inductive Teaching of English*, Cooperative Research Program, U. S. Office of Education, U. S. Department of Health, Education, and Welfare, Project No. H-015, 1967.

Vygotsky, L. S. *Thought and Language*. Translated by Eugenia Hanfmann and Gertrude Vakar. New York: M. I. T. Press and John Wiley and Sons, 1962.

Whitehead, Alfred North. *Process and Reality*. New York: Macmillan, 1929, 31-38.

White, Morton. *The Age of Analysis*. New York: Mentor Books, 1929, 31-38.

Woods Hole Preliminary Report. *The Process of Education*. Report of the Conference on Fundamental Processes in Education. Woods Hole, Massachusetts: National Academy of Sciences, 1959.